T0158954

A Synopsis of the Epistles
of the APOSTLE PAUL
by Sciphre Institute

DIRECTOR ERNEST L. BRANNON

WESTBOW
P R E S S®
A DIVISION OF THOMAS NELSON
& ZONDERVAN

Scripture taken from the King James Version of the Bible.

WestBow Press books may be ordered through booksellers or by contacting:

WestBow Press
A Division of Thomas Nelson & Zondervan
1663 Liberty Drive
Bloomington, IN 47403
www.westbowpress.com
1 (866) 928-1240

ISBN: 978-1-5127-9653-7 (sc)
ISBN: 978-1-5127-9654-4 (e)

Library of Congress Control Number: 2017911281

Print information available on the last page.

WestBow Press rev. date: 7/31/2017

The Epistles of the Apostle Paul is a summary of the letters that Paul wrote to the church as the body of Christ. The commentary was transcribed by Dr. Ernest Brannon, a retired professor in biology, and director of the Sciphre Institute. The institute supports Campus Crusade for Christ by promoting a balanced forum in science, philosophy, and religion on the university campus. The synopsis of Paul's epistles is a contribution of the spiritual element of that endeavor.

Dedicated to my treasure

CONTENTS

Preface xi

Acknowledgments... xv

Background on Paul's Epistles.......................xvii

Romans 1

1 Corinthians... 18

2 Corinthians...34

Galatians... 41

Ephesians...52

Philippians 69

Colossians 79

1 Thessalonians 88

2 Thessalonians 98

Pastoral Epistles 106

1 Timothy.. 108

2 Timothy 115

Titus.. 121

Philemon... 124

Hebrews.. 126

Retrospect 137

PREFACE

These synopses of the epistles of Paul have been prepared as an overview of his timely instructions to Christians. Using the Holy Bible: King James Version, Cleveland, Ohio, The World Publishing Company, 1945, the synopsis gives a summary perspective of Paul's letters in preparation for a more in-depth study of his writings. They are not a substitute for those books in the Bible but are meant as a general overview of their revelations.

It is important to understand the purpose of the epistles. Humans were created to fellowship with God, but they were given the freedom to make the choice to accept or reject such fellowship. In the course of events that followed, humans disobeyed God, which separated them from that fellowship and destined them to an existence apart from God called eternal death. Paul's objective was to communicate the gospel of Jesus Christ, the Messiah or Savior, who came to redeem humanity from that condition. His epistles were letters to the churches that sought his advice or counseling as the body of believers on that matter.

Separation from God is characterized as unrighteousness, which manifests as sinful acts. God, in his perfect countenance, cannot tolerate the presence of sin, but in his grace, God provided a plan for man's redemption. That plan requires a sacrifice involving the letting of blood, signifying the source of life, as an offering to amend for man's sinful nature. The ritual that God designated in his covenant with the Israelites in the Old Testament was to offer the blood of animals on the altar of their worship. That offering was an ongoing oblation for their sins, but those sacrifices did not take away the sin nature, nor did they provide salvation from the penalty of death. The blood of animals was only a surrogate for the cleansing blood that was to eventually come through the Messiah. Jesus was that Messiah, the Son of God sent for the redemption of man. When Christ shed his blood on the cross, he provided a permanent sacrifice for the redemption of man's sinful nature. Those who choose to embrace the gift of redemption are said to be born again and are "saved"—saved from eternal death.

Paul is very thorough in communicating the reality of the sin nature in man and exposing the false doctrines that were causing the spiritual problems that existed in the early church. Many of those problems are still apparent in the post-modern church. Paul was explicit in his message explaining salvation, the Christian walk, and our reconciliation with God when we stumble. The journey through Paul's epistles is a compelling and rewarding experience in the Christian life. He invites us to join the faith and use our talents for the glory of God as the Spirit leads.

ACKNOWLEDGMENTS

Many thanks to Nancy Payne for the editing of the manuscript and for her helpful suggestions.

BACKGROUND ON PAUL'S EPISTLES

Paul wrote the majority of the letters of the New Testament. It is the Lord's instruction through Paul that revealed the mystery of who constituted the children of God and the revelation that those children are referred to as the body of Christ, the church. His letters develop church doctrine—the order, position, principles, and duties of that body—and they confirm that Jesus Christ, as the head of the church, is the savior that God sent to redeem man from the penalty of sin.

God called Paul as his apostle, and unlike the other apostles, Paul had been taught in the religious schools of the Hebrews. He was a Pharisee and a Roman and thus was very knowledgeable of the Old Testament scriptures and the prophecies concerning the coming Messiah (Isaiah 7, 9, 25, 42, and 53). But he didn't know Christ was that Messiah until it was revealed by Jesus himself when Paul was confronted by our Lord on the road to Damascus (Acts 9).

Paul, as a zealot for the Jewish faith, had persecuted the Jewish converts to Christ, hunting them down and taking them before the high priest to be cast into prison or put to death. But on the road to Damascus all of that changed. Jesus confronted Paul and said, *"Saul, Saul, why persecutest thou me?"* After recognizing Jesus, Paul said, *"Lord what will you have me to do?"*

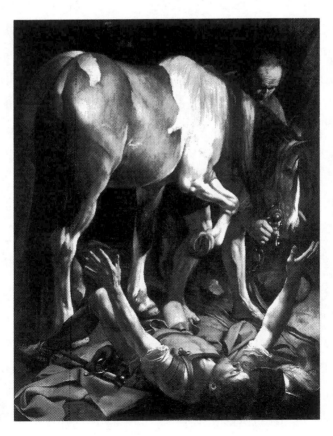

That moment was Paul's conversion experience. After his conversion, Paul went into Arabia and later returned to Damascus, involving a span of three years in which he learned of the truth of God's plan for man from the revelations communicated by Christ himself (Galatians 1:11–12). When the disciples heard of Paul's conversion, they were dubious, and even the apostles feared him. But Paul's testimony convinced them that he was a convert to Christ.

Recall that at the time Paul wrote his letters there was no New Testament. Even the first gospel had not yet been written, and Paul had no instruction from the other apostles. It is apparent that Paul acquired his knowledge of God's plan directly from Christ, and his message was the essence of God's truth regarding faith and the promises that were in store for those who believed.

We now turn to the letters of Paul and examine their message. The synopsis is presented in the sequence of the epistles that appear in the Bible.

ROMANS

Romans is a letter Paul wrote to the believers in Rome during his last visit to Corinth around AD 60. The letter was prepared in anticipation of his visit to the center of the world empire at that time. Although written as a letter to the Roman church, it is universal in that it defines the Christian faith and affirms the doctrine of salvation by grace. The promises of God encompass both Jews and Gentiles as the one body of Christ, and it was Paul's intent to make sure there were no questions about those basic principles of Christianity Jesus revealed to him.

Rome was essentially pagan, but the Jews were sufficient in number to have been one of the focal points for Paul. Much of the letter to the Romans is in reference to the Jews and their special place in the plan of God. However, the Jews were also the legalistic teachers who assailed the gospel, and thus they presented a major challenge for Paul's outreach to the unbelievers and for his instruction to the church about righteousness.

His message was the essence of God's truth regarding faith and the promises that were in store for those who believed. That message can be divided in six parts: (1) introduction, (2) state of humanity, (3) moral distinctions, (4) God's justice and provision, (5) Israel's covenant, and (6) Christian behavior.

1) In his introduction, Paul shows that Jesus fulfilled the Old Testament prophecies that stated that the Messiah was to come via the seed of David (2 Samuel 7:8–17), and that the Son of God would overcome death (Isaiah 25:8). He said, *"Concerning his Son Jesus Christ our Lord, which was made of the seed of David according to the flesh; And declared to be the Son of God with power, according to the spirit of holiness, by the resurrection from the dead"* (Romans 1:3–4).

It is noteworthy that Paul used the reference to "the seed of David according to the flesh." It is apparent that the Jews were an important part of the Roman believers and would identify with the prophecies in the Old Testament scriptures. The phrase "according to the flesh" is a reference to the prophetic lineage of David for both Mary and Joseph, which is distinct from the actual divine origin as the seed of God. It appears that the Gentile members of the Roman church were also aware of those prophecies.

Paul is writing to both barbarians and Greeks—to the wise and the unwise, including the Jews. *"For I am not ashamed of the gospel of Christ: for it is the power of God unto salvation to everyone that believeth; to the Jew first, and also to the Greek. For therein is the righteousness of God revealed from faith to faith: as it is written, The just shall live by faith"* (Romans 1:16–17).

Paul's primary message is that righteousness can come only by faith in Jesus, who came to redeem humankind from unrighteousness. That is the promise of God—and it is the promise of salvation—to both the Jew and the Gentile. It was apparent that Paul's message to the Roman Christians had the secondary purpose of addressing the need for repentance in the culture of the Gentile pagan empire, the center of worldly passions and greed. His epistle to the Romans had application as a universal message well beyond just Roman believers.

2) Paul starts his commentary on the retribution that is to fall upon the wickedness of humankind by addressing the state of the intelligentsia— those educated Greeks who took pride in their own wisdom and rejected God as the source of that wisdom. He refers to them as those who fall among the ungodly and unrighteous in spite of the evidence of God, and thus they are recipients of God's wrath. He says, *"For the wrath of God is revealed from heaven against all ungodliness and unrighteousness of men, who hold the truth in unrighteousness; Because that which may be known of God is manifest in them; for God hath shewed it unto them. For the invisible things of him from the creation of the world are clearly seen, being understood by the things that are made, even his eternal power and Godhead; so that they are without excuse"* (Romans 1:18–20).

Paul left no doubt about the unbelieving intelligentsia. God was evident everywhere around them, but they chose not to recognize the Creator and instead worshiped things of the world. That was the situation in Rome, where worldly knowledge was supreme and immorality was even applauded. Paul put it in spiritual perspective. Those who believed in such things were left to their uncleanness—to dishonor their own bodies in unspeakable lusts worthy of death. The worldly culture of Rome was the pathway to destruction, and the expanding presence of that pathway is very evident in the world today.

Paul also addresses those who thought themselves superior and above the common person. He speaks of those who judge and in so doing actually condemn themselves because they are guilty of the same offenses. He says, *"Therefore thou art inexcusable, O man, whosoever thou art that judgest: for wherein thou judgest another, thou condemnest thyself; for thou that judgest doest the same things"* (Romans 2:1). God will render to every person according to his or her deeds. The state of the natural person, Jew or Gentile, is a state of unrighteousness in the eyes of God—but it is a state that can be overcome by faith and obedience to God.

3) In moral distinctions, Paul makes it clear that God is impartial to the individual and fair in his judgment. Gentiles who are not under the law will perish because of their sin. But for those Gentiles who obey the things of the law, they show the works of the law in their hearts. In contrast, for those Jews who were circumcised in obedience to the covenant with God but were really not

committed to God in their heart, their circumcision is of no worth. Paul says the commitment of the heart is what counts, not the outward pretense. Simply put, Gentiles and Jews are seen as the same by God if both are committed in their hearts to the things of God. They are called the children of God. If they are not committed, then they both suffer the same consequences.

If that is the case, what advantage has the Jew? Paul says "much" because the Jews were given the oracles of God and chosen as the vehicle through which Christ would be communicated to the world. While the apostles as Jews carried out that responsibility, the Jews as a people failed to do so, to their greater condemnation.

Paul says that Jews and Gentiles alike are under sin and that none are righteous. *"Therefore by the deeds of the law there shall no flesh be justified in his sight: for by the law is the knowledge of sin"* (Romans 3:20). Paul leaves no uncertainty about the law. Its purpose was meant to make the Jews aware of sin. The law did not provide a means to salvation, which would come only by being declared as righteous, and the law effectively demonstrated that humans were incapable of being righteous.

4) Paul then turns to God's justice and says, *"For all have sinned, and come short of the glory of God; Being justified freely by his grace through the redemption that is in Christ Jesus: … To declare, I say, at this time his righteousness: that he might be just, and the justifier of him which believeth in Jesus"* (Romans 3:23–26).

Jesus was designated by God to be the means of atoning for sin by his sacrifice on the cross. Through that sacrifice—the death of the Son of God on the cross—justice for all of the past and future sins of humanity was provided for by God. That provision was the atonement made for sin, which was sufficient for all time.

But Paul makes it clear that God's provision was more than atonement for sin. By the resurrection of Christ, the believer is also raised to life eternal through faith and made righteous in the eyes of God. If we accept by faith that Christ died for us, we can be confident that we are redeemed unto lives of righteousness. Paul says any attempt to be righteous by our own effort is futile. He retorts, *"Where is boasting then? It is excluded. By what law? of works? Nay: but by the law of faith. Therefore we conclude that a man is justified by faith without the deeds of the law. … Do we then make void the law through faith? God forbid: yea, we establish the law"* (Romans 3:27–31).

The law was fulfilled by Christ. While the law was meant to reveal what constituted righteousness and show that humanity was incapable of obeying the law to achieve righteousness, individuals can attain the state of righteousness through Christ's righteousness. When we accept Christ as Savior, we are redeemed by the blood he shed for us. If people try to earn their own righteousness, then they will fail—because no one is made righteous through his or her own effort. Only those who accept our Savior into their hearts are counted as righteous by the grace of God.

As an example, Paul refers to Abraham, who received his seal of righteousness by his faith in God long before the law was given through Moses—and even before the Jewish covenant was made through circumcision. Therefore, Abraham is viewed as the father of all those, whether Jew or Gentile, who are justified by faith through the grace of God.

We should now continue at peace with God, knowing that we are forgiven by God's grace. We should exult in the hope of that divine promise of eternal life that God has given through Jesus; we are saved and reconciled with God by the living Christ. Sin entered the world through the disobedience of one man—Adam—and death prevailed for the whole human race. But through one man, Jesus Christ, those who receive God's gift of righteousness have overcome death and have the promise of eternal life by the grace of God. Our separation from God through Adam's disobedience was more than overcome by God's grace. The gift of reunification with God came through the one man, our Lord Jesus Christ.

To receive that gift, one only needs to accept it with a heartfelt faith. Paul makes it clear. *"That if thou shalt confess with thy mouth the Lord Jesus, and shalt believe in thine heart that God hath raised him from the dead, thou shalt be saved. For with the heart man believeth unto righteousness; and with the mouth confession is made unto salvation. ... For whosoever shall call upon the name of the Lord shall be saved"* (Romans 10:9–13).

Baptism symbolizes our death with Jesus and rising again with him to live a new life. *"Knowing this, that our old man is crucified with him, that the body of sin might be destroyed, that henceforth we should not serve sin. … Neither yield ye your members as instruments of unrighteousness unto sin: but yield yourselves unto God, as those that are alive from the dead, and your members as instruments of righteousness unto God"* (Romans 6:6–13).

Paul continues, *"But now being made free from sin, and become servants to God, ye have your fruit unto holiness, and the end everlasting life. For the wages of sin is death; but the gift of God is eternal life through Jesus Christ our Lord"* (Romans 6:22–23). Therefore, as believers in Christ, we are no longer servants of sin, because as Christians we are cleansed of sin in the eyes of God. However, sin still abides in the human flesh, and as long as we have our present bodies, we will stumble with sin, but when we stumble, the Holy Spirit will reveal our mistakes and prompt us of our error. By yielding to God, we can then ask for forgiveness and to repent from such failures.

Paul then returns to the Jew under the law. In Christ the Jew is dead to the law, because he has the newness of life provided by the Savior. Paul says of himself that he did not know sin until the law revealed his own carnal nature. Paul goes on to say that he knows to do good, but his human nature doesn't allow him to perform as he should.

Rather the sin that he knows he should not do, he does. He attributes this to the will of the flesh. But he says that with Christ in his life, he now possesses the Holy Spirit, which has overcome the will of the flesh and allows him to live a life that can abstain from that sin.

The conclusion of the matter is this: there is no condemnation for those who are united with Christ Jesus. What the law could not do because of the nature of man, God has done by coming as a sinless man who died as a perfect sacrifice to redeem us from sin. Therefore, as Christians we are free from the bondage of sin, and the Spirit of God reassures us that we are his children. As children, we are heirs of God's glory that is beyond the ability of the human mind to fully comprehend. Salvation is the promise of God, and that is our hope, for now unseen, but secured by our faith.

Paul says, *"And we know that all things work together for good to them that love God, to them who are the called according to his purpose. For whom he did foreknow, he also did predestinate to be conformed to the image of his Son ... and whom he called, them he also justified: and whom he justified, them he also glorified"* (Romans 8:28–30).

God is timeless and knows the future as he knows the past. In that capacity, he predestined the course of those who accepted Christ as Savior to be like Christ, and thus to have the holiness of Christ as their example in this life. Jesus sits at the right hand of the throne of God and pleads our case. There is no force that can separate us from the love of God in Christ Jesus our Lord.

5) God remembers his covenant with the Jews and has not abandoned Israel. As a Jew himself, Paul longs to have his kinfolk saved. Israel's history is rich with the splendor of the divine presence, the patriarchs, the covenant, temple worship, and the promises. But those born in the line of Abraham through the course of nature are not necessarily God's children, but rather only those who are born through God's promise; both Jew and Gentile who accept Jesus as Savior are the children of God. Those Jews who sought after the law and rejected the promised Messiah—Christ—were blinded to the gospel. God then turned to the Gentiles to carry the gospel to the lost, but they too are failing by turning from Christ.

Paul says, *"Hath not the potter power over the clay, of the same lump to make one vessel unto honour, and another unto dishonour?"* (Romans 9:21).

God tolerated those vessels designated for dishonor to show his mercy. Both Jew and Gentile are those vessels. The Jews didn't recognize the Messiah or his message and continued after the law. The Gentiles recognized Christ's claim as the redeemer, but they failed to overcome the attractiveness of the present world. But Paul is not cast down and still sees the promises and the greater truth.

Paul asks, *"Hath God cast away his people? God forbid ... but rather through their fall salvation is come unto the Gentiles"* (Romans 11:1,11). But Paul warns the Gentiles not to feel superior and uses the natural olive tree as the metaphor, saying, *"And if the root be holy, so are the branches. And if some of the branches be broken off* [meaning the unbelieving Jews], *and thou, being a wild olive tree,* [meaning the Gentiles], *wert graffed in among them, and with them partakest of the root and fatness of the olive tree; Boast not against the branches ... because of unbelief they were broken off, and thou standest by faith. Be not highminded, but fear: For if God spared not the natural branches, take heed lest he also spare not thee ... And they also, if they abide not still in unbelief, shall be graffed in: for God is able to graff them in again"* (Romans 11:16–23).

Paul says be not ignorant of the fact that the blindness will have happened to Israel until the time of the Gentiles is completed, and then Israel will have their eyes opened and the truth revealed. Israel had fallen because of their lack of faith, but they are still the elect of God. When the Gentiles were unbelieving, God showed them mercy. The same is true for the Jews. God's purpose is to show his mercy for all humankind.

We can only conclude with Paul, *"O the depth of the riches both of the wisdom and knowledge of God! how unsearchable are his judgments, and his ways past finding out! For who hath known the mind of the Lord? or who has been his counselor? ... For of him, and through him, and to him, are all things: to whom be glory for ever. Amen"* (Romans 11:33–36).

6) Paul then turns to Christian behavior. He says, *"I beseech you therefore, brethren, by the mercies of God, that ye present your bodies a living sacrifice, holy, acceptable unto God, which is your reasonable service. And be not conformed to this world: but be ye transformed by the renewing of your mind, that ye may prove what is that good, and acceptable, and perfect, will of God"* (Romans 12:1–2). Paul makes the point that

although we are in the spirit, we are still subject to the wants of the flesh and personally must turn from such desires and give priority to serving the Lord.

We are not to think more highly of ourselves than what we deserve and recognize that God has given us our measure of faith. The gifts that are given differ among the brethren according to the grace that God has allotted, whether prophecy, preaching, giving, charity, teaching, or such. We, as brethren, are members of the body, each given gifts and a special responsibility to join with the rest of the body using those gifts to serve God. We are to reach out to the less fortunate, love both the brethren and those that reject us, rejoice in hope, be patient in tribulation, continue in an instant in prayer, be fervent in spirit, and be not wise in our own conceits.

We are to be subject to authority that God has instituted and approved, and we are to respect the authority as God ordained. We are to pay our taxes and leave no outstanding debt to any man. All such commandments are summed up in one rule, and that is to love your neighbor as yourself. The whole law is fulfilled by love.

We are told to be prepared for Christ's return. Awake out of your sleep and throw off the deeds of darkness; no revealing or petty arguments, or even jealousies. Give no thought to satisfying bodily appetites. Put on the armor of Christ. We will have to answer for ourselves as we stand before God's tribunal. As Christians we belong to Christ. We are no longer to live for ourselves, but for the Lord. Don't cause weak brothers to fail by your poor example or judgment. If God has accepted the weak brother, who are we to judge him or to put an obstacle in his way? Accept one another as Christ accepted us, to the glory of God.

In completing the synopsis of Paul's letter to the Romans, it is important to emphasize the critical point. As Christians we are seen by God as sinless. God sees the believer as sinless, not because of our good behavior or works, but simply because we accept Christ as our Savior who died in our place to redeem us from our sinful state. However, we are still susceptible to sin because we remain in our body of flesh until we are given new bodies at the second coming of Christ. That is why Paul told the Roman Christians to adapt themselves no longer to the pattern of this world, but to allow the Spirit to live within them and direct their paths. This does not come automatically. While we as Christians are free from the bondage of sin, we must be vigilant and put on the armor of Christ against the ways of the world through prayer and allowing the Spirit to reign in our lives to honor God. We are to love our fellow man and to abstain from the unrighteousness of sinful behavior, including even such things as gossip that can hurt those that God loves.

The key verse:

Romans 10:13: *"For whosoever shall call upon the name of the Lord shall be saved."*

1 CORINTHIANS

Paul's first letter to the Corinthians was written around AD 56. Corinth was an important port for trade with Italy and the west, as well as with Asia Minor. Consequently, the city had great wealth and luxury, including the arts, but was also infamous for vice and immorality. Paul had established the church in Corinth on his second missionary journey during a two-year visit to the city. Church membership was primarily made up of Gentiles, but Jews had witnessed the church in action. Those Jews who came to the knowledge of Christ were part of the Corinthian church.

The epistle was written from Ephesus in response to a letter from the Corinth Christians asking questions about marriage and the eating of meat offered to idols, but Paul's objective was to address much more than that. Specifically he wanted to deal with an instance of carnality within that body. In this respect the Corinthians represented contrasts in the faith, similar to the Christian culture we experience today.

Paul felt some in the church were well grounded in the faith and said, *"I thank my God always on your behalf, for the grace of God which is given you by Jesus Christ; That in every thing ye are enriched by him, in all utterance, and in all knowledge; Even as the testimony of Christ was confirmed in you: So that ye come behind in no gift; waiting for the coming of our Lord Jesus Christ"* (1 Cor. 1:4–7). So he affirmed that many in the church were faithful in their commitment to the gospel of Christ and were enriched in knowledge of the Lord, even in exercising the gifts of the Spirit.

This was in contrast to what Paul also saw as the influence of Greek learning and philosophy on the believers. Some members demonstrated pride and lauded secular pursuits. They were well off and enjoyed the luxuries of their society, which affected their character. Paul addresses nine issues, including their questions. (1) Divisions among the believers, (2) incest, (3) lawsuits, (4) fornication, (5) answers to questions, (6) abuse of the Lord's supper, (7) gifts of the Spirit (8) affirmation of the gospel, and (9) raising of the dead.

1) Paul first addressed the divisions and factions that had occurred within the body after he had

founded the church. Some were identifying with Paul, while others were following Apollos or Peter, and still others recognized only Christ. Paul said, *"Is Christ divided?"* (1 Corinthians 1:13). Paul made it clear that such factions were childish, that the body was under the head of Christ, and there should be no divisions—only unity.

Paul goes on to explain that the problem is pride in their wealth, conceit about their knowledge, and their identity with leaders in the ministry rather than Christ and the cross. Paul said these were traits of the worldly, leading to destruction. He then identifies the source of the problem. *"For the preaching of the cross is to them that perish foolishness; but unto us which are saved it is the power of God ... For the Jews require a sign, and the Greeks seek after wisdom: But we preach Christ crucified, unto the Jews a stumbling block, and unto the Greeks foolishness"* (1 Corinthians 1:18, 22–23).

The Jews didn't recognize Jesus as the Messiah and could not reconcile their expectation of a king with someone they perceived to be a taunting commoner. And the Greeks could not accept the humility that their wisdom was worthless compared to the cross that was to redeem them from a life of sin. This was the problem with the Corinthian church—they were influenced by the carnality of the society around them.

Paul puts that in perspective and explains that the natural man does not understand the spiritual things of God because such knowledge requires spiritual discernment, which is lacking without spiritual birth. God chose what the world counts as weakness to demonstrate that there is no place for human pride in the presence of God. With those that have heard God's call, Christ demonstrates God's power and wisdom.

Paul continues, *"Howbeit we speak wisdom among them that are perfect: yet not the wisdom of this world, nor of the princes of this world, that come to naught: But we speak the wisdom of God in a mystery, even the hidden wisdom, which God ordained before the world unto our glory: Which none of the princes of this world knew: for had they known it, they would not have crucified the Lord of glory. But as it is written, Eye hath not seen, nor ear heard, neither have entered into the heart of man, the things which God hath prepared for them that love him. But God hath revealed them unto us by his Spirit: for the Spirit searcheth all things, yea, the deep things of God"* (1 Corinthians 2:6–10).

Although Paul commended the Corinthians for their knowledge of the truth of Christ, he went on to say, *"And I, brethren, could not speak unto you as unto spiritual, but as unto carnal, even as unto babes in Christ. I have fed you with milk, and not with meat: for hitherto ye were not able to bear it, ... For ye are yet carnal: for whereas there is among you envying, and strife, and divisions, are ye not carnal, and walk as men? For while one saith, I am of Paul; and another, I am of Apollos; are ye not carnal? Who then is Paul, and who is Apollos, but ministers by whom ye believed, even as the Lord gave to every man? I have planted, Apollos watered; but God gave the increase. So then neither is he that planteth any thing, neither he that watereth; but God that giveth the increase. Now he that planteth and he that watereth are one: and every man shall receive his own reward according to his own labour"* (1 Corinthians 3:1–8).

Paul was telling the Corinthians that they were still infants in understanding God's word and had let materialism influence their thinking. The illustration was to show that there are no human icons, only Christ. Paul, Apollos, and Peter were only stewards of Christ fulfilling each of their responsibilities. It was the Spirit of God in Christ that was the power to be recognized.

Using the illustration of a building, Paul said that he laid the foundation of Jesus Christ and others will build upon that foundation, but there is no other foundation beyond on which eternity is based. Paul reminds the Corinthians that as Christians their work will be judged by God, and thus their stewardship, including any false pride or material lust will be rewarded accordingly. They are now the temple of the Holy Spirit, and that is the foundation on which they are to build.

Paul emphasizes the point of false pride. He says, *"For who maketh thee to differ from another? and what hast thou that thou didst not receive? now if thou didst receive it, why dost thou glory, as if thou hadst not received it?"* (1 Corinthians 4:7). Be humble and recognize your abilities are God given.

2) Next, Paul reprimands the Corinthians for their tolerance of incest, in the case of a union of a man in the church with his father's wife, which he said wouldn't be tolerated even by the pagans. The man should have been rooted out of the congregation and treated in a manner that would

cause him to repent and be saved in the Day of the Lord. They were to have nothing to do with any Christian that behaves in such a manner.

3) Paul then reprimands the Corinthians for their readiness to take each other to pagan courts of law and to attempt to redress their grievances in the presence of unbelievers that have no spiritual discernment. *"I speak to your shame. Is it so, that there is not a wise man among you? no, not one that shall be able to judge between his brethren?"* (1 Cor. 6:5). Paul said it would be better to suffer loss than to abuse a brother. He relates such behavior to that of the unjust who will never enter the kingdom of God. As Christians they must realize they are members of the body dedicated to God and to deal with such issues as brothers, justified in the name of the Lord Jesus and the Spirit of our God. Therefore they were to act accordingly.

4) Even further, Paul refers to those that say, "I am free to do anything." But not everything is for good. Certainly their tolerance of incest was an issue they should have been ashamed of. He says, *"A little leaven leaveneth the whole lump"* (1 Corinthians 5:6). Tolerance and indulgence of immorality of a few affected the testimony of them

all. He told them to shun fornication. *"What? know ye not that your body is the temple of the Holy Ghost which is in you, which ye have of God, and ye are not your own?"* (1 Corinthians 6:19).

5) Paul then answers the Corinthians' questions. The first was about marriage. He said each man can have a wife and each woman a husband, both of whom should consider their bodies not their own but belonging to the other. If one dies, the other is free to remarry. God's ruling is that divorce should not be undertaken. Paul then gives his own advice that widows and the unmarried should stay as they are in order to serve God, if they are so inclined. For those with an unsaved mate, Paul tells them to live in peace with their spouse, because they never know how their behavior might bring the partner to a saving belief. But if the unsaved partner seeks a separation, the Christian is under no compulsion to continue in the marriage.

Concerning food consecrated to heathen deities, Paul told the Corinthians that a Christian is free to consume meat as he or she may choose, because the Christian knows there is but one God, and consecrating meat to idols does nothing to the meat. But a Christian should be sensitive to the weaker brother who might be offended by eating meat consecrated to idols. In that case, he or she should abstain in order to respect the believer who is at a different level of understanding. Confusing a weaker brother by insisting on our right to do something would be a sin against that brother, and also against Christ.

6) Paul then addresses the Corinthians' manner of worship, which had become disordered. The traditions he preached about should be followed. God is the head of Christ, and Christ is the head of man. In turn man is the head of his wife. According to the custom of the day, men should not cover their heads in prayer, in order to show their respect to God. But it was appropriate for a woman to cover her head as an indication that she respected her husband's position of authority.

But a greater problem of their worship was in their behavior when they came together at the Lord's supper. He charged them with scandalous disorder where they gorged themselves with food and drink, rather than partaking in the observance of the blood and body that Christ sacrificed on the cross. He said, *"What? have ye not houses to eat and to drink in? or despise ye the church of God, and shame them that have not? ... Wherefore whosoever shall eat this bread, and drink this cup of the Lord, unworthily, shall be guilty of the body and blood of the Lord. But let a man examine himself, and so let him eat of that bread, and drink of that cup"* (1 Corinthians 11:22, 27–28). Paul said they were to partake as a memorial to Christ.

7) Paul then turns to the gifts of the Spirit. The Corinthians were rich in gifts, but it appears that some were amiss in how they exercised their gifts. He told them that no one could say by the Spirit that Jesus was accursed, and no one could say that Jesus was Lord except that the Spirit was in their heart. Spiritual gifts come from God and are to be used for him. Some are to encourage salvation, others are for instruction. The gifts vary, and in each of us the Spirit is manifested in a particular way. Some have the gift of wisdom, others the gift of knowledge, or the gift of faith, or the gift of healing, or the gift of miracles, or the gift of prophecy, or the gift of discerning the spirits, or the gift of different tongues or the interpretation of tongues among others, but all the gifts are given by the same Spirit of God, who distributes them separately to each individual at will. The body of Christ is made up of many members, and they must be united together in their work. Not

all are prophets, not all are healers or teachers, but the body works as one, and if one suffers, all will suffer, and if one flourishes, all will rejoice together. We are to desire the best gifts.

We can assume that the Corinthians were guilty of pride in the exercise of their gifts, but Paul says there is a more excellent way to function, and that is with love. A person can have great gifts, but if he has not love, those gifts amount to nothing.

He then defines love or charity: *"Charity suffereth long, and is kind; charity envieth not; charity vaunteth not itself, is not puffed up, Doth not behave itself unseemly, seeketh not her own, is not easily provoked, thinketh no evil; Rejoiceth not in inequity, but rejoiceth in the truth; Beareth all things, believeth all things, hopeth all things, endureth all things. Charity never faileth"* (1 Corinthians 13:4–8). Paul says that the gifts will come to an end, but faith, hope, and love will abide forever, and the greatest of these is love.

The Corinthians appear to have put great worth in the speaking of tongues, and while Paul didn't discourage tongues, he said he would rather they prophesy. Speaking in unknown tongues was not speaking to man, but speaking to God. The unknown tongues are a mystery to men because no one understands the tongue unless there is an interpreter. Prophecy is for the edification, exhortation, and comfort of men and the edification of the church. They are told to seek that which edifies the church, and if a man speaks in tongues, pray that it will be interpreted.

Paul says, *"Brethren, be not children in understanding: howbeit in malice be ye children, but in understanding be men ... If therefore the whole church be come together into one place, and all speak with tongues, and there come in those that are unlearned, or unbelievers, will they not say that ye are mad? But if all prophesy, and there come in one that believeth not, or one unlearned, he is convinced of all, he judged of all: And thus are the secrets of his heart made manifest; and so falling down on his face he will worship God, and report that God is in you of a truth ... Wherefore, brethren, covet to prophesy, and forbid not to speak with tongues. Let all things be done decently and in order"* (1 Corinthians 14:20, 23–25, 39–40).

It is apparent that Paul's emphasis on prophecy was not to minimize the other gifts, but it was to demonstrate the vivid contrast between tongues and those gifts that could be seen to edify the church. The Corinthians had been divided into groups, each acting separate from the others.

Speaking in tongues had been exercised to the extreme and most likely given elevated status. Paul put it in perspective by preaching that the body of the church should be unified in using their gifts to edify the church for the glory of God.

8) The subject then turns to the affirmation of the gospel. After the rather severe admonition that he gave the Corinthians, Paul reiterated the gospel story to remind the church body about the promises of God and life after death. Some in the church didn't believe that Christ was raised from the dead, so Paul made it very clear what was at stake.

"Christ died for our sins according to the scriptures; And that he was buried, and that he rose again the third day according to the scriptures: And that he was seen of Cephas, then of the twelve: After that, he was seen of above five hundred brethren at once … After that, he was seen of James; then of all the apostles. And last of all he was seen of me also … Now if Christ be preached that he rose from the dead, how say some among you that there

is no resurrection of the dead? But if there be no resurrection of the dead, then is Christ not risen: And if Christ be not risen, then is our preaching vain, and your faith is also vain ... If in this life only we have hope in Christ, we are of all men most miserable" (1 Corinthians 15:3–8, 12–14, 19).

Paul said that death came as a consequence of Adam's sin, but Christ's redeeming sacrifice made life available to us as members of the kingdom of God. And when the end comes, Christ will deliver up the kingdom to God, after abolishing all worldly authority. God has put all enemies under Christ's feet, and death will be the last enemy to be destroyed. Paul said, *"And when all things shall be subdued unto him, then shall the Son also himself be subject unto him that put all things under him, that God may be all in all"* (1 Corinthians 15:28).

9) Finally, the Corinthians apparently asked in their letter about how the dead were raised and in what body would they appear. Paul said it was a foolish question, but he answered: *"Thou fool, that which thou sowest is not quickened, except it die: And that which thou sowest, thou sowest not that body that shall be ... It is sown in corruption; it is raised in incorruption: It is sown in dishonour; it is raised in glory: it is sown in weakness; it is raised*

in power: It is sown a natural body; it is raised as a spiritual body" (1 Corinthians 15:36–37, 42–44). Paul made it clear that the body we now have will be replaced with a new body when Christ returns. We have been in the likeness of man made from dust, but we will be like the heavenly man in the Spirit. *"Death is swallowed up in victory. O death, where is thy sting? … The sting of death is sin; and the strength of sin is the law. But thanks be to God, which giveth us the victory through our Lord Jesus Christ"* (1 Corinthians 15:54–57).

The key verse

1 Corinthians 15:58: *"Therefore, my beloved brethren, be ye stedfast, unmovable, always abounding in the work of the Lord, forasmuch as ye know that your labour is not in vain in the Lord."*

2 CORINTHIANS

The second epistle Paul wrote to the Corinthians is thought to have been written about a year after Paul's first epistle. Although Paul had planned to visit Corinth as indicated in 1 Corinthians, it appears that he delayed his visit. The reason he gave was that he didn't want to come to them again in heaviness, apparently referring to his first letter where he reprimanded them for carnal behavior on several issues.

As in other epistles, Paul greets them saying, *"Grace be to you and peace from God our Father, and from the Lord Jesus Christ"* (2 Corinthians 1:2), a reference indicating that he is speaking on God's behalf. Further, he says, *"Who comforteth us in all our tribulation, that we may be able to comfort them which are in any trouble, by the comfort wherewith we ourselves are comforted of God"* (2 Corinthians 1:4).

Paul then recounts the serious troubles that confronted his ministry in Asia Minor—so severe that they even despaired of life. He says this happened to teach them not to place reliance on themselves, but on God, who is able to raise the dead. Paul says that God delivered them and he will deliver them again, and he acknowledged the Corinthians for their prayers from such despair, there will be many to thank for the care of God.

Paul's first letter to the Corinthians came out of his great distress and anxiety, with tears as he wrote it. He meant no pain to result from that letter, but rather he wanted them to know of his love for them. However, because of that concern, Paul delayed his second visit until he could come with commendation, and in the meantime, he wrote the second letter relating to four issues that were preliminary to his visit: (1) To commend them for the manner in which they dealt with the problem of incest, (2) to reaffirm his commitment, (3) to secure support for the poor, and (4) then to vindicate his apostleship authority.

1) In advance of his visit, Paul commends them for how they handled the problem of incest and other issues. They took to heart all of the things Paul had said to them, recognizing his authority. Paul says that something different is now called for. *"So that contrariwise ye ought rather to forgive him, and comfort him, lest perhaps such a one should be swallowed up with overmuch sorrow. Wherefore I beseech you that ye would confirm your love toward him"* (2 Corinthians 2:7–8).

2) Paul then speaks of the commitment that he and those accompanying him have given in God's ministry. This appears meant to reassure them that Paul recognizes their faithfulness to Christ. *"Ye are our epistle written in our hearts, known and read of all men: Forasmuch as ye are manifestly declared to be the epistle of Christ ministered by us, written not with ink, but with the Spirit of the living God; not in tables of stone, but in fleshy tables of the heart"* (2 Corinthians 3:2–3).

Paul says it is his full reliance upon God, through Christ, that enables him to make such a claim. He says that the law written on stone revealed the sin that resulted in our condemnation and death. But through the new covenant of Christ, we are forgiven. The old covenant was nullified by Christ, and the splendor of the new covenant endures forever. Paul says we reflect the splendor of the Lord, because we are transfigured into his likeness as we are more and more influenced by his Spirit.

In reference to his own work, Paul says it is not by his power but by the power of God alone that enables him to speak the truth and not distort the word of God. He says he is only as an earthen vessel that contains the transcendent power that comes only from God. He and his workmen are continually surrendering to the threat of death for the sake of Jesus Christ, so that the life of Jesus may also be revealed in their mortal bodies.

"For the love of Christ constraineth us; because we thus judge, that if one died for all, then were all dead: And that he died for all, that they which live should not henceforth live unto themselves, but unto him which died for them, and rose again ... Therefore if any man be in Christ, he is a new creature: old things are passed away; behold, all things are become new. And all things are of God, who hath reconciled us to himself by Jesus Christ, and hath given to us the ministry of reconciliation; To wit, that God was in Christ, reconciling the world unto himself, not imputing their trespasses

unto them; and hath committed unto us the word of reconciliation ... For he hath made him to be sin for us, who knew no sin; that we might be made the righteousness of God in him. We then, as workers together with him, beseech you also that ye receive not the grace of God in vain" (2 Corinthians 5:14—6:1). Paul emphasized that they were not to give offense to anything, but to function as ministers of God in all circumstances with much patience. He told the Corinthians they would be afflicted, but they were to stay steadfast in their commitment.

His talk was frank, but he felt their hearts were not totally open to his message. Apparently some of the members of the church had aligned themselves with unbelievers who spoke against Paul's authority and maintained idol worship. He urged them not to unite with those people, and to come out from among them. *"Having therefore these promises, dearly beloved, let us cleanse ourselves from all filthiness of the flesh and spirit, perfecting holiness in the fear of God"* (2 Corinthians 7:1).

He asked those who still felt wronged to make a place in their heart for him and his companions. He was encouraged by the report of Titus who said the Corinthians took his letter seriously, in Paul's support. Paul said the believers had been awakened to see justice done, and they had vindicated themselves from all blame in the trouble that had beset their church.

3) The subject then turns to the issue of contributing aid to those Christians in need. Paul used the generosity of the congregations in Macedonia as an example and asked the Corinthians to have their promised contribution ready when he arrived. He reminded them, *"God loveth a cheerful giver"* (2 Corinthians 9:7).

4) The last of this epistle addresses claims made by sham-apostles that Paul was morally weak. They claimed equal or superior apostolic authority and complained that Paul encroached upon the areas in which other Christian leaders had built congregations. Paul denied this and said his authority to preach the gospel was commissioned by Christ and verified by the signs, marvels, and miracles in his ministry. He warned about the sham-apostles. *"For such are false apostles, deceitful workers, transforming themselves into the apostles of Christ. And no marvel; for Satan himself is transformed into an angel of light"* (2 Corinthians 11:13–14).

Paul finishes by saying that when he comes he fears that he will find some among them that have woefully sinned and not repented. He says, *"Examine yourselves, whether ye be in the faith; prove your own selves. Know ye not your own selves, how that Jesus Christ is in you ... Now I pray to God that ye do no evil; not that we should appear approved, but that ye should do that which is honest, ... For we can do nothing against the truth, but for the truth"* (2 Corinthians 13:5–8).

The key verse:

2 Corinthians 5:17: *"Therefore if any man be in Christ, he is a new creature: old things are passed away; behold, all things are become new."*

GALATIANS

The apostle Paul wrote this letter sometime after AD 50. It was written from Corinth after Paul's first missionary journey to the churches of Galatia, which included more than one fellowship in Asia Minor, presently dominated by the nation of Turkey. The residents were primarily Gauls and apparently came to Christ under Paul's first or second missionary journey.

The Gauls were largely of Celtic origin, and unlike the Celtic tribes north of the Alps those living in Asia Minor at the time of Christ had integrated more with Roman culture. Thus while the gospel was a revelation of an entirely new life to the Galatians, they were also susceptible to false teaching.

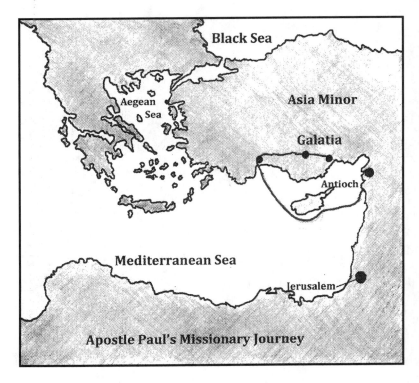

Apostle Paul's Missionary Journey

Paul had become aware that the Galatians were led to integrate Jewish law with faith in Christ as the foundation of Christianity. The problem was caused by certain Jews, referred to as the Nicolaitans, who claimed to follow Christ, but were preaching a different gospel than what Paul had taught when the churches in Galatia were established. They taught that: (1) keeping the Mosaic law mingled with faith was the grounds for the forgiveness of sin and thus eternal life, and (2) that the believer is made perfect by keeping the law. Apparently, this was a problem that several of the churches were experiencing.

1) Paul wrote to refute the teachings of the Nicolaitans. He said: *"I marvel that ye are so soon removed from him that called you into the grace of Christ unto another gospel ... But I certify you, brethren, that the gospel which was preached of me is not after man. For I neither received it of man, neither was I taught it, but by the revelation of Jesus Christ ... But when it pleased God, who separated me from my mother's womb, and called me by his grace, To reveal his Son in me, that I might preach him among the heathen; immediately I conferred not with flesh and blood"* (Galatians 1:6–16).

Paul, as a Jew, previously a committed Pharisee educated under the Mosaic law, wrote: *"We who are Jews by nature, and not sinners of the Gentiles, Knowing that a man is not justified by the works of the law, but by the faith of Jesus Christ, even we have believed in Jesus Christ, that we might be justified by the faith of Christ, and not by the works of the law: for by the works of the law shall no flesh be justified"* (Galatians 2:15–16).

Paul makes it clear that the law does not save the soul. This truth is underscored by Paul pointing out that he too, as an apostle, put his faith in Christ in order to be justified. He says: *"But if, while we seek to be justified by Christ, we ourselves also are found sinners, is therefore Christ the minister of sin? God forbid. For if I build again the things I destroyed, I make myself a transgressor. For I through the law am dead to the law, that I might live unto God. I am crucified with Christ: nevertheless I live; yet not I, but Christ liveth in me: and the life which I now live in the flesh I live by the faith of the Son of God, who loved me, and gave himself for me. I do not frustrate the grace of God: for if righteousness come by law, then Christ is dead in vain"* (Galatians 2:17–21).

2) Paul then returns to the topic of the Nicolaitans' teaching. He says: *"O foolish Galatians, who hath bewitched you, that ye should not obey the truth, before whose eyes Jesus Christ hath been evidently set forth, crucified among you? This only would I learn of you, Received ye the Spirit by the works of the law, or by the hearing of faith? Are ye so foolish? Having begun in the Spirit, are ye now made perfect by the flesh? Have ye suffered so many things in vain? if it be yet in vain. He therefore that ministereth to you the Spirit,*

and worketh miracles among you, doeth he it by the works of the law, or by the hearing of faith?" (Galatians 3:1–5).

So here Paul contrasts the law and the gospel with regard to salvation and the working of the Holy Spirit in perfection. He asked the Galatians how they could now include the material law when they originally left the material for the spiritual. He asked them to look at the great experiences they'd had in coming to the knowledge of Christ and the salvation for all eternity. Had those experiences now been in vain?

He reminded them about Abraham and used Abraham as an example of faith, a faith God counted as righteousness, and Abraham predated the law given to Moses by 430 years. The point was that Abraham's righteousness was not secured by the law but by faith. The Jews had missed that truth, and that error was being exaggerated by the Nicolaitans' teachings.

God gave Abraham the promise that faith in the coming Messiah is what makes a person righteous and erases sins. It is not a legal right assumed by the Jews. The law had a specific purpose, and that was to point out the offense of sin. *"For if the inheritance be of the law, it is no more of promise: but God gave it to Abraham by promise. Wherefore then serveth the law? It was added because of transgressions, till the seed should come to whom the promise was made; and it was ordained by angels in the hand of a mediator"* (Galatians 3:18–19).

Paul emphasizes the point by showing that the law and the promises were different in their purpose. He continues: *"Is the law then against the promises of God? God forbid: for if there had been a law given which could have given life, verily righteousness should have been by the law. But the scripture hath concluded all under sin, that the promise by faith of Jesus Christ might be given to them that believe. But before faith came, we were kept under the law, shut up unto the faith which should afterwards be revealed. Wherefore the law was our schoolmaster to bring us unto Christ, that we might be justified by faith. But after that faith is come, we are no longer under a schoolmaster. For ye are all the children of God by faith in Christ Jesus. For as many of you as have been baptized into Christ have put on Christ. There is neither Jew nor Greek, there is neither bond nor free, there is neither male nor female: for ye are all one in Christ Jesus. And if ye be Christ's, then are ye Abraham's seed, and heirs according to the promise"* (Galatians 3:21–29).

Paul points out the problem that the Galatians, are being led by the Nicolaitans to revert back to something they were burdened with before they became Christians. Paul underscores the fact that Jewish traditions will not bring redemption: *"But now, after that ye have known God, or rather are known of God, how turn ye again to the weak and beggarly elements, whereunto ye desire again to be in bondage? Ye observe days, and months, and times, and years. I am afraid of you, lest I have bestowed upon you labour in vain"* (Galatians 4:9–11).

Paul tells the Galatians that when they accepted Christ they entered into the saving promises of God, and now they are being diverted from knowing the truth. *"Ye did run well; who did hinder you that ye should not obey the truth? This persuasion cometh not of him that calleth you. A little leaven leaveneth the whole lump. I have confidence in you through the Lord, that ye will be none otherwise minded: but he that troubleth you shall bear his judgment, whosoever he be"* (Galatians 5:7–10).

Paul reminds the Galatians that Christ made them free, but now through false teaching they are returning to captivity. *"For, brethren, ye have been called unto liberty; only use not liberty for an occasion to the flesh, but by love serve one another. For all the law is fulfilled in one word, even in this; Thou shalt love thy neighbour as thyself. But if ye bite and devour one another, take heed that ye be not consumed one of another. This I say then, Walk in the Spirit, and ye shall not fulfil the lust of the flesh. For the flesh lusteth against the Spirit, and the Spirit against the flesh: and these are contrary the one to the other: so that ye cannot do the things that ye would. But if ye be led of the Spirit, ye are not under the law"* (Galatians 5:13–18).

Paul then refers to some of the behaviors that characterize the lower nature of man contrary to love. *"Now the works of the flesh are manifest, which are these; Adultery, fornication, uncleanness, lasciviousness, Idolatry, witchcraft, hatred, variance, emulations, wrath, strife, seditions, heresies, Envyings, murders, drunkenness, revellings, and such like: of the which I tell you before, as I have also told you in time past, that they which do such things shall not inherit the kingdom of God"* (Galatians 5:19–21).

He then presents the traits of the new man in Christ. *"But the fruit of the Spirit is love, joy, peace, longsuffering, gentleness, goodness, faith, Meekness, temperance: against such there is no law. And they that are Christ's have crucified the flesh with the affections and lusts. If we live in the Spirit, let us also walk in the Spirit"* (Galatians 5:22–25).

The truth is that if we submit our will to Jesus, our lives will reflect those characteristics via the power of the Holy Spirit.

Finally, Paul covers the outworking of the new life. *"Brethren, if a man be overtaken in a fault, ye which are spiritual, restore such an one in the spirit of meekness; considering thyself, lest thou also be tempted. Bear ye one another's burdens, and so fulfill the law of Christ. For if a man think himself to be something, when he is nothing, he deceiveth himself ... Be not deceived; God is not mocked: for whatsoever a man soweth, that he shall also reap"* (Galatians 6:1–3,7).

God's promises are not complicated. Salvation is simply a matter of faith. It is not based on our goodness or compassion for others, even though that is part of Christian character. Because of the nature of man, natural man always generates a system of laws and regulations that he believes are the prescription for salvation. That in essence is the history of the church. Laws and regulations prescribing behavior undermine the truth that only faith is required.

That is what the Nicolaitans were guilty of when they preached to the Galatians that Moses's law continues to be necessary, but Paul said the law no longer applies. Yes, Christians are to behave in a manner that glorifies God, but that is the fruit of abiding in Christ and being subject to the directions given through the Holy Spirit. When we accept Christ as Savior, we have died with Christ and rise with him to a new life, a life led by Christ.

As Paul testified, *"I am crucified with Christ: nevertheless I live; yet not I, but Christ liveth in me: and the life which I now live in the flesh I live by the faith of the Son of God, who loved me, and gave himself for me"* (Galatians 2:20).

That is the key to a productive and peaceful life as servants of our Lord. He will direct our paths as we seek to serve him. If we are vigilant in waiting upon God to show us what he wants to do through us, we will be able to use the gifts and the talents he gave us for his glory, rather than trying to decide for ourselves what we should do. Be aware of your gifts, and use them to glorify our Lord.

The key verse:

Galatians 5:1: *"Stand fast therefore in the liberty wherewith Christ hath made us free, and be not entangled again with the yolk of bondage."*

EPHESIANS

Ephesians is believed to have been the first of the prison letters from Rome and was written about AD 62, along with the letters to the Colossians and Philippians. There is some question whether it might have been addressed to the church at Laodicea rather than Ephesus, since the best manuscripts apparently didn't mention to whom it was addressed, and the Colossians were asked to share their letter with the Laodiceans and vice versa (Colossians 4:16), but no such letter addressed to the Laodiceans has been found. So while the King James Bible identifies the Ephesians as the intended recipients, the history is uncertain. The essential point, however, is that the letter was written to the body of Christ, not just the local congregation, and it was meant to have a wide impersonal audience in which the highest church truth was communicated.

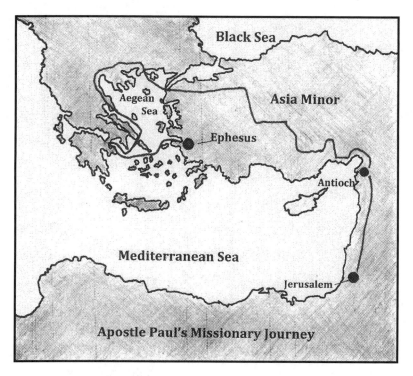

On his second missionary journey, Paul visited with the Ephesians and entered the synagogue to talk with the Jews (Acts 18:19). On his next visit, he met with the disciples of John the Baptist and said to them, *"Have ye received the Holy Ghost since ye believed? And they said unto him, We have not so much as heard whether there be any Holy Ghost. And he said unto them, Unto what then were you baptized? And they said, Unto John's baptism. Then said Paul, John verily baptized with the baptism of repentance, saying unto the people, that they should believe on him*

which should come after him, that is, on Christ Jesus. When they heard this, they were baptized in the name of the Lord Jesus" (Acts 19:2–5).

In his epistle, Paul defines the principles of the Christian faith by presenting three lines of truth: (1) the believer's exalted position through grace, (2) the body of Christ, and (3) the Christian walk.

1) On the first Paul leaves no uncertainty about the ultimate future in Christ, the eternal joy when we enter the unity of heaven, and the new earth under grace. God predestined believers to be holy in Christ even before the creation of the world. With God there is no time. He knows the future as he knows the past. Foreknowledge is no mystery for God. Paul says, *"Blessed be the God and Father of our Lord Jesus Christ, who hath blessed us with all spiritual blessings in heavenly places in Christ: According as he hath chosen us in him before the foundation of the world, that we should be holy and without blame before him in love: Having predestinated us unto the adoption of children by Jesus Chris to himself, according to the good pleasure of his will, To the praise of the glory of his grace, wherein he hath made us accepted in the beloved. In whom we have redemption through his blood, the forgiveness of*

sins, according to the riches of his grace; Wherein he hath abounded toward us in all wisdom and prudence; Having made known unto us the mystery of his will, according to his good pleasure which he hath purposed in himself: That in the dispensation of the fullness of times he might gather together in one all things in Christ, both which are in heaven, and which are on earth; even in him" (Ephesians 1:3–10).

Paul continues to discuss the grace of God and the believer's position. He says, *"In whom also we have obtained an inheritance, being predestinated according to the purpose of him who worketh all things after the counsel of his own will: That we should be to the praise of his glory, who first trusted in Christ. In whom ye also trusted, after that ye heard the word of truth, the gospel of your salvation: in whom also after that ye believed, ye were sealed with that holy Spirit of promise, Which is the earnest of our inheritance until the redemption of the purchased possession, unto the praise of his glory ... The eyes of your understanding being enlightened; that ye may know what is the hope of his calling, and what the riches of the glory of his inheritance in the saints, And what is the exceeding greatness of his power to us-ward who believe, according to the working of his mighty power"* (Ephesians 1:11–19).

So while the Jews rejected Christ, the apostles, who were the first to hope in Christ, turned to include the Gentiles in the family of God. They were given the same gospel of salvation through the blood of Christ. It was predestined in God's plan that the Jews and Gentiles be one in our Lord Jesus Christ. Consequently, the Gentiles who became Christians have the riches of God's glorious inheritance and his incomparably great power as believers, the same as believing Jews.

Reference to predestination of the believers is noteworthy in that it has been a controversial issue among Bible commentators. This has been mistakenly interpreted to mean that a given person is predestined to be saved, but that is contrary to the doctrine of free choice. Predestination in Paul's letter doesn't apply to the individual, but rather to the body. In love he predestined the body of believers to be holy and adopted as his sons through Jesus Christ. Sons is plural, not singular, meaning the brotherhood. Thus the individual determines by free will whether he or she chooses to be included in that body, the true church.

Also noteworthy is the statement that we are sealed with the Holy Spirit, guaranteeing our inheritance. Guaranteeing our inheritance reaffirms the eternal security of the believer that is presented in Hebrews 13:5, where Paul, referring to Jesus, said, *"For he hath said, I will never leave thee nor forsake thee."* And in John 10:27–29 he said, *"My sheep hear my voice, and I know them, and they follow me: And I give unto them eternal life; and they shall never perish, neither shall any man pluck them out of my hand."*

Paul goes on to say that God placed all things under the feet of Christ and appointed him to be head over everything in the church. We have been given God's mercy as members of the true church, but he reminds the Ephesians what they were before: *"And you hath he quickened, who were dead in trespasses and sins; Wherein in time past ye walked according to the course of this world, according to the prince of the power of air, the spirit that now worketh in the children of disobedience: Among whom also we all had our conversation in times past in the lusts of our flesh, fulfilling the desires of the flesh and of the mind; and were by nature the children of wrath, even as others"* (Ephesians 2:1–3).

Paul then shows how that fatal worldly condition of fallen man was transformed by the grace of God into life everlasting through redemption in Christ by God's mercy. *"But God, who is rich in mercy, for his great love wherewith he loved us, Even when we were dead in sins, hath quickened us together with Christ, (by grace ye are saved;) And hath raised us up together, and made us sit together in heavenly places in Christ Jesus: That in the ages to come he might shew the exceeding riches of his grace in his kindness toward us through Christ Jesus"* (Ephesians 2:4–7).

Paul leaves no doubt about who gets credit for salvation. It was provided by the grace of God. However, it is the exercise of one's free choice to accept or reject God's grace. That is the key. A person's good intentions or charitable works provide no passage to eternal life. Paul says, *"For by grace are ye saved through faith; and that not of yourselves: it is the gift of God: Not of works, lest any man should boast. For we are his workmanship, created in Christ Jesus unto good works, which God hath before ordained that we should walk in them"* (Ephesians 2:8–10).

Paul makes it plain. It is Christ's redeeming grace that saves us; it is not our righteousness. But once we accept Christ as Savior, from that point on God expects us to have good works, and they are counted in our service to him. Without the blood of Christ on the cross, our righteousness would be as filthy rags (Isaiah 64:6), but when we accept Christ as Savior, we accept his death in our place, and in the eyes of God we are made righteous and worthy. We are to walk accordingly.

2) The second topic, which follows naturally from the first, is about the body of Christ. Paul tells the Ephesian Gentiles that they had been separated from God, excluded from citizenship in Israel, and foreigners to the covenants of the promise, without hope and without God in the world. But in Christ Jesus they who once were far away as Gentiles have been brought near through the blood of Christ. Now, in Christ, the Gentiles and Jews are both members of the body of Christ.

Paul emphasizes this point about the membership in the body of believers, and the concept that the believer now is the temple of the Holy Spirit. *"Now therefore ye are no more strangers and foreigners, but fellowcitizens with the saints, and of the household of God; And are built upon the foundation of the apostles and prophets, Jesus Christ himself being the chief corner stone; In whom all the building fitly framed together groweth unto an holy temple in the Lord: In whom ye also are builded together for an habitation of God through the Spirit"* (Ephesians 2:19–22).

Paul said that the mystery kept from the world up to that time was that the Gentiles were to be fellow-heirs with the Jews and of the same body as partakers of Christ so Christ may dwell in their hearts by faith, being rooted and grounded in love. So the Gentiles were predestined to be included among the children of God. That was a revelation to the Christian Jews. The Gentiles would no longer be outcast in their eyes but rather were to become one people with them.

Paul then refers to how these believers are to walk and to serve in the body: *"I therefore, the prisoner of the Lord, beseech you that ye walk worthy of the vocation wherewith ye are called, With all lowliness and meekness, with longsuffering, forbearing one another in love; Endeavoring to keep the unity of the Spirit in the bond of peace. There is one body, and one Spirit, even as ye are called in one hope of your calling; One Lord, one faith, one baptism, One God and Father of all, who is above all, and through all, and in you all"* (Ephesians 4:1–6).

So the mystery was not only that Gentiles and Jews were one people, but they were also one body, the true church, in which there were many members with different gifts for God's service. Paul says that God's grace varies among the believers, and with that grace came the different gifts for the unity of the Spirit.

"But unto every one of us is given grace according to the measure of the gift of Christ ... And he gave some, apostles; and some, prophets; and some, evangelists; and some, pastors and teachers; For the perfecting of the saints, for the work of the ministry, for the edifying of the body of Christ: Till we all come in the unity of the faith, and of the knowledge of the Son of God, unto a perfect man, unto the measure of the stature of the fullness of Christ" (Ephesians 4:7–13).

Maturity in Christ means we will no longer be infants, tossed back and forth by every new philosophy taught by deceitful men. Instead, speaking the truth in love, we will grow up by following the example of Christ, and thus as we are committed to our particular calling, we will function in unity of the body for God's glory.

3) The third topic concerns the walk and service of the believer. Once we become the children of God, it is here that works now count. We are to be obedient to Christ, and our behavior is to reflect the Lord in our lives. That is what God expects of us in our calling to serve him.

Paul says, "This I say therefore, *and testify in the Lord, that ye henceforth walk not as other Gentiles walk, in the vanity of their mind, Having the understanding darkened, being alienated from the life of God through the ignorance that is in them, because of the blindness of their heart: Who being past feeling have given themselves over unto lasciviousness, to work all uncleanness with greediness"* (Ephesians 4:17–19).

Paul's description of how the Gentiles lived is in effect how the world continues to live to this day. Materialism has characterized society throughout the ages and remains a challenge to Christian society. What the church disapproved of as worldly behavior a few years ago is to a large extent endured by the church today. Paul provides the essence of how believers should conduct themselves by listing the appropriate behavior that is becoming to the Christian.

"That ye put off concerning the former conversation the old man, which is corrupt according to the deceitful lusts; And be renewed in the spirit of your mind; And that ye put on the new man, which after God is created in righteousness and true holiness. Wherefore putting away lying, speak every man truth with his neighbour: for we are members one of another. Be ye angry, and sin not: let not the sun go down upon your wrath: Neither give place to the devil. Let him that stole steal no more: but rather let him labour, working with his hands the thing which is good, that he may have to give to him that needeth. Let no corrupt communication proceed out of your mouth, but that which is good to the use of edifying, that it may minister grace unto the hearers. And grieve not the holy Spirit of God, whereby ye are sealed unto the day of redemption. Let all bitterness, and wrath, and anger, and clamour, and evil speaking, be put away from you, with all malic: And be ye kind one to another, tenderhearted, forgiving one another, even as God for Christ's sake hath forgiven you" (Ephesians 4:22–32).

Paul then turns to a note of caution about those things that are to be avoided. He says, *"For this ye know, that no whoremonger, nor unclean person, nor covetous man, who is an idolater, hath any inheritance in the kingdom of Christ and of God. Let no man deceive you with vain words: for because of these things cometh the wrath of God upon the children of disobedience. Be not ye therefore partakers with them. For ye were sometimes darkness, but now are ye light in the Lord: walk as children of light: (For the fruit of the Spirit is in all goodness and righteousness and truth;) Proving what is acceptable unto the Lord. ... Wherefore be ye not unwise, but understanding what the will of the Lord is. ... Giving thanks always for all things unto God and the Father in the name of our Lord Jesus Christ"* (Ephesians 5:5–10, 17, 20).

We are to love our spouse and submit to one another out of reverence for Christ. In love husband and wife join together and become one flesh. Paul describes this as a profound mystery, but it is a model of Christ and the church. We are to love our children, and they are to honor their parents. Fathers are responsible for bringing up the children in the training and instruction of the Lord.

Finally, Paul underscores the source of evil that the Christian must fight against using the means of defense that God makes available to his children. This is a critical element in the life of the Christian. There is a war going on, but it is not the war against unbelievers. Paul describes the warring forces and the defense. *"Finally, my brethren, be strong in the Lord, and in the power of his might ... For we wrestle not against flesh and blood, but against principalities, against powers, against the rulers of the darkness of this world, against spiritual wickedness in high places. Wherefore take unto you the whole armour of God, that ye may be able to withstand in the evil day, and having done all, to stand. Stand therefore, having your loins girt about with truth, and having on the breastplate of righteousness; And your feet shod with the preparation of the gospel of peace; Above all, taking the shield of faith, wherewith ye shall be able to quench all the fiery darts of the wicked. And take the helmet of salvation, and the sword of the Spirit, which is the word of God: Praying always with all prayer and supplication in the Spirit, and watching thereunto with all perseverance and supplication for all saints"* (Ephesians 6:10–18).

It is apparent that the letter to the Ephesians was not meant for a given local church, but most certainly was meant to be instructive to the body of believers throughout Christendom. Paul succinctly lays out the Christian truth that our goodness or works mean nothing regarding our salvation. God's grace is what allows man to become a child of God. When God came to man in the form of man, the Messiah, and offered himself on the cross to redeem humankind separated from God by disobedience (sin), it was the grace of God that allowed man the free choice to reunite with God, not by man's goodness. Accepting Christ as Savior was all man had to do to experience renewed life and to fellowship with God forever.

Christians as members of the body—the church—with Christ at the head, who followed in the shadow of Jesus, were expected to exhibit lives full of good works. The mystery that was revealed in this letter was that God predestined the Gentiles to be part of the body of believers identified as the children of God. And just as the Jews were to honor God in their service and worship, so too were the Gentiles to honor and serve God in a manner fitting for the fellowship for which God created man.

It is instructive to look at the spiritual succession of the Ephesians, or the Laodiceans, as a warning to the church denominations that are becoming more secularized. Just thirty years after Paul commended these believers for their faith (Ephesians 1:15–16), they had fallen away from that faith. Jesus, speaking through the Revelation of John, told the Ephesians: *"Nevertheless I have somewhat against thee, because thou hast left thy first love. Remember therefore from whence thou are fallen"* (Revelation 2:4–5). And to the Laodiceans he said, *"I know thy works, that thou art neither cold nor hot: I would thou wert cold or hot. So then because thou are lukewarm, and neither cold nor hot, I will spue thee out of my mouth"* (Revelation 3:15–16).

These two churches were among the seven addressed in Revelation. They had not held true to their walk in Christ and were on the verge of condemnation in just one generation after their founding. It represents a strong warning about the vulnerability of the church to stray from the fundamentals taught by Christ.

The key verse:

Ephesians 1:13: *"In whom ye also trusted, after that ye heard the word of truth, the gospel of your salvation: in whom also after that ye believed, ye were sealed with that holy Spirit of promise."*

PHILIPPIANS

The letter to the Philippians, like the letters to the Colossians and the Ephesians, was written by Paul while he was imprisoned in Rome, around AD 62.

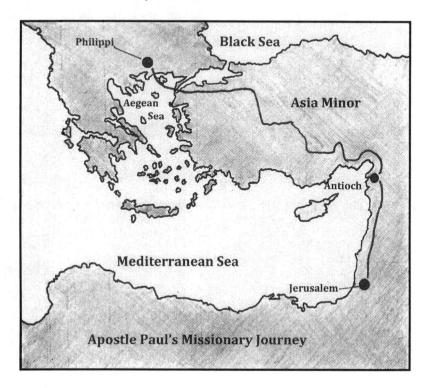

During Paul's second journey into Asia Minor, he was called in a vision to cross the Aegean Sea to Macedonia to help the Gentile believers in that region. The congregation at Philippi was the first that Paul refers to on that missionary trip, which was a substantial journey along the northern and western territories bordering the Aegean Sea.

Philippians is a letter unlike Paul's others letters in that he didn't write to reprimand the church. Rather he wrote a letter of brotherly love to the people who were very dear to him, thanking them for their diligence in the faith, assuring them of his spiritual victory in spite of imprisonment, and communicating about their life in Christ. He also told them how much he appreciated their faithfulness in their support of his ministry.

His letter covers five topics associated with Christ and the expectations of the believer: (1) prayer for discernment, (2) victory through affliction, (3) being of one mind, (4) the sufficiency, and (5) the joy of service.

1) He starts with a prayer for their discernment to increase in love and to advance in the fruit of righteousness by following the direction of the Spirit of Christ to the glory of God. *"And this I pray,*

that your love may abound yet more and more in knowledge and in all judgment; That ye may approve things that are excellent; that ye may be sincere and without offence till the day of Christ; Being filled with the fruits of righteousness, which are by Jesus Christ, unto the glory and praise of God" (Philippians 1:9–11).

2) Paul's second point was that victory can be achieved through affliction. Paul stated that his prison time was not wasted but rather used for good in that it reached even the palace residents associated with his confinement. He says, *"But I would ye should understand, brethren, that the things which happened unto me have fallen out rather unto the furtherance of the gospel; So that my bonds in Christ are manifest in all the palace, and in all other places; And many of the brethren in the Lord, waxing confident by my bonds, are much more bold to speak the word without fear"* (Philippians 1:12–14).

Paul was in chains, attached to a guard, but had freedom to receive guests and to instruct those around him concerning Jesus as recorded in Acts 28:16, 20, 30 where we read Luke's account as follows: *"And when we came to Rome, the centurion delivered the prisoners to the captain of the guard: but Paul was suffered to dwell by himself with a soldier that kept him ... For this cause therefore have I called for you, to see you, and to speak with you: because that for the hope of Israel I am bound with this chain ... And Paul dwelt two whole years in his own hired house, and received all that came in unto him."*

Not only did Paul's testimony reach the palace guard but also their headquarters, the palace leaders, and the public at large. This emboldened his brothers to testify of Jesus as well. Victory came through Paul's incarceration, and he rejoiced that Christ was set forth. He knew the Spirit of Jesus Christ and the prayers of the Philippians were supporting him, and that Christ would be exalted in Paul's body, whether by life or by death.

Then he delivered his well-known verse: *"For to me to live is Christ, and to die is gain" (*Philippians 1:21). This confirmed that while Paul desired to depart to the Lord, he knew it was more necessary that he continue with his ministry, and it would involve tribulation. This was consistent with his message about what the believer would also experience. Paul spoke of victory through affliction. Even in the face of conflict, believers were to conduct themselves in a manner worthy of the gospel of Christ regardless of the challenge—not to be frightened by those who opposed their witness, but to stand firm in one spirit, contending together as one for the faith of the gospel. This would be a sign to those who deny the truth of Christ that the gospel resonates with conviction and not being frightened in any way by the consequences. God has granted on behalf of Christ the rewards of believing on him, but also to suffer for him when facing tribulation.

3) The third point was to be likeminded in Christ. Paul said if they had any comfort from Christ's love, any fellowship with the Spirit, any tenderness and compassion, then: *"Fulfil ye my joy, that ye be likeminded, having the same love, being of one accord, of one mind. Let nothing be done through strife or vainglory; but in lowliness of mind let each esteem other better than themselves. Look not every man on his own things, but every man also on the things of others"* (Philippians 2:2–4).

Paul leaves no doubt that God came as Christ in the form of man, was obedient to death for us, and now he is in heaven as our redeemer, and as our redeemer we are to be like him. This is only possible by depending on the presence of the Holy Spirit.

He says, *"Let this mind be in you, which was in Christ Jesus: Who, being in the form of God, thought it not robbery to be equal with God: But made himself of no reputation, and took upon him the form of a servant, and was made in the likeness of men: And being found in fashion as a man, he humbled himself, and became obedient unto death, even the death of the cross. Wherefore God also hath highly exalted him, and given him a name which is above every name: That at the name of Jesus every knee should bow, of things in heaven, and things in earth, and things under the earth; And that every tongue should confess that Jesus Christ is Lord, to the glory of God the Father"* (Philippians 2:5–11).

Paul then says something that has become a source of controversy: *"Work out your own salvation with fear and trembling. For it is God which worketh in you both to will and to do of his good pleasure. Do all things without murmurings and disputings: That ye may be blameless and harmless, the sons of God, without rebuke, in the midst of a crooked and perverse nation, among whom ye shine as lights in the world"* (Philippians 2:12–15).

Some have felt the verses imply that salvation is by works, but in reality those verses mean that

Philippians

in our saved state as the children of God we are to work through the tasks God has called us to perform. The Christian must pay attention to his or her calling. That is what "working out" means.

4) The fourth point was the sufficiency of Christ. Paul tells the believers to watch out for those who advocated the need for circumcision (and thus the law) to attain one's salvation. He implies that those who are the followers of Christ are already circumcised, because in their hearts they worship Christ Jesus through the Spirit and do not put their trust in fleshly obedience. If there were such reasons for status in the flesh, Paul says it would most certainly apply to him: *"Circumcised the eighth day, of the stock of Israel, of the tribe of Benjamin, an Hebrew of the Hebrews; as touching the law, a Pharisee; Concerning zeal, persecuting the church; Touching the righteousness which is in the law, blameless"* (Philippians 3:5–6).

But Paul said that whatever he profited by obeying Jewish law and tradition, he now considered of no value compared to the gains found in following Christ. His righteousness now comes not from the law but by his faith in Christ. The power of Christ's resurrection gives Paul the courage to suffer for Christ's sake. Paul's active pursuit of

Philippians

Christ-likeness was an example to the Philippians that such a pursuit was to be an ongoing activity of the Christian.

Paul related, *"Not as though I had already attained, either were already perfect: but I follow after, if that I may apprehend that for which I also am apprehended of Christ Jesus. Brethren, I count not myself to have apprehended: but this one thing I do, forgetting those things which are behind, and reaching forth unto those things which are before, I press toward the mark for the prize of the high calling of God in Christ Jesus. Let us therefore, as many as be perfect, be thus minded: and if in any thing ye be otherwise minded, God shall reveal even this unto you. Nevertheless, whereto we have already attained, let us walk by the same rule, let us mind the same thing. Brethren, be followers together of me, and mark them which walk so as ye have us for an ensample. (For many walk, of whom I have told you often, and now tell you even weeping, that they are the enemies of the cross of Christ: Whose end is destruction, whose God is their belly, and whose glory is in their shame, who mind earthly things.) For our conversation is in heaven; from whence also we look for the Saviour, the Lord Jesus Christ: Who shall change our vile body, that it may be fashioned like unto his glorious body, according to the working whereby he is able even to subdue all things unto himself"* (Philippians 3:12–21).

While that message to believers is an encouragement to concentrate on our high calling of God in Jesus Christ, and to put in proper perspective the life we now experience in Christ, it is also sober instruction that the believer should no longer be drawn to the vices of this world.

5) Paul's fifth topic was joy in service. *"Rejoice in the Lord alway: and again I say, Rejoice. Let your moderation be known unto all men. The Lord is at hand. Be careful for nothing; but in every thing by prayer and supplication with thanksgiving let your requests be made known unto God. And the peace of God, which passeth all understanding, shall keep your hearts and minds through Christ Jesus"* (Philippians 4:4–7). These instructions of Paul to the Philippians are applicable to the church today. We are to surrender our will to God, and thus submit to the presence of the Holly Spirit to guide our thoughts and actions. Prayer and study of God's word is the critical part of that process.

Paul then finishes by saying, *"Finally, brethren, whatsoever things are true, whatsoever things are honest, whatsoever things are just, whatsoever things are pure, whatsoever things are lovely, whatsoever things are of good report; if there be any virtue, and if there be any praise, think on these things. Those things, which ye have both learned, and received, and heard, and seen in me, do: and the God of peace shall be with you"* (Philippians 4:8–9).

The Key Verse:

Philippians 4:13: *"I can do all things through Christ which strengtheneth me."*

COLOSSIANS

Colosse was a church located in Asia Minor, and apparently established by Epaphras, but never actually visited by Paul. With Ephesians and Philippians, Colossians was one of Paul's three prison letters. It was written sometime around AD 62 and very compassionately expresses Paul's recognition of the Colossians' faith in Christ.

The population of Colosse was diverse and largely Gentile. However, Antiochus III had settled Jewish families in the general area in 213 BC, leaving a strong Jewish minority still present around the city. Contributing to its diversity and rich cultural history was its location near the great Persian Royal Road that ran from Ephesus 120 miles in the West to the Euphrates and on to Persia in the East.

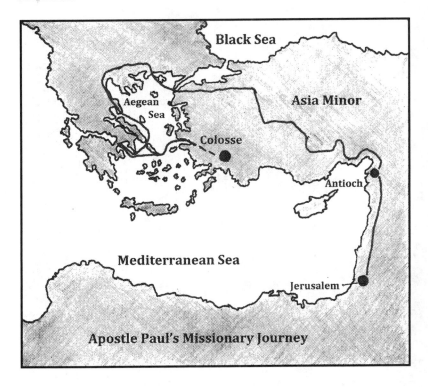

Apostle Paul's Missionary Journey

Paul wrote to the Christians of Colosse to thwart the influence of the cult called the Gnostics. The cult taught that more was involved in salvation than just accepting Christ, and that the simple forms of worship were inadequate. They claimed that a deeper spiritual experience required further hidden and secret knowledge that only their loyal followers could acquire. This was not a strange situation in Colosse, since it was situated on a major trade route from the East that had a steady stream of Oriental visiting traders with mysterious religious ideas. Paul doesn't waste time on the heresy. Rather than refuting the cult worship by addressing each of the false teachings, and thus giving them prominence by naming them and discussing the errant philosophy, Paul simply emphasized that Jesus Christ was totally adequate in all respects, and that only faith in him was necessary. There are no other requirements in a deeper spiritual life than submitting to Christ. Four points were emphasized: (1) knowledge of God, (2) the position of God's children, (3) the mystery, and (4) Christian behavior.

1) After his greeting, Paul refers to the knowledge and wisdom available to the believers through their faith and life in Christ, as well as their responsibility to use it as children of God. He thus indirectly confronts the issue of this spiritual heresy. He says, *"For this cause we also, since the day we heard it, do not cease to pray for you, and to desire that ye might be filled with the knowledge of his will in all wisdom and spiritual understanding; That ye might walk worthy of the Lord unto all pleasing, being fruitful in every good work, and increasing in the knowledge of God; Strengthened with all might, according to his glorious power, unto all patience and longsuffering with joyfulness; Giving thanks unto the Father, which hath made us meet to be partakers of the inheritance of the saints in*

light: Who hath delivered us from the power of darkness, and hath translated us into the kingdom of his dear Son: In whom we have redemption through his blood, even the forgiveness of sins" (Colossians 1:9–14).

Paul makes it very clear that Jesus is everything in both the spiritual and the physical world. Without him nothing would exist. This was a truth that the Gnostics could not deal with because they didn't understand the totality of Christ.

Paul referring to Christ says, *"Who is the image of the invisible God, the firstborn of every creature: For by him were all things created, that are in heaven, and that are in earth, visible and invisible, whether they be thrones, or dominions, or principalities, or powers: all things were created by him, and for him: And he is before all things, and by him all things consist. And he is the head of the body, the church: who is the beginning, the firstborn from the dead; that in all things he might have the preeminence. For it pleased the Father that in him should all fullness dwell; And, having made peace through the blood of his cross, by him to reconcile all things unto himself; by him, I say, whether they be things in earth, or things in heaven"* (Colossians 1:15–20).

2) Paul follows this by reference to the unique position of the children of God for which he is now their minister of their growth in Christ. He says, *"And you, that were sometime alienated and enemies in your mind by wicked works, yet now hath he reconciled In the body of his flesh through death, to present you holy and unblameable and unreproveable in his sight: If you continue in the faith grounded and settled, and be not moved away from the hope the gospel, which ye have heard, and which was preached to every creature which is under heaven; whereof I Paul am made a minister"* (Colossians 1:21–23).

3) Paul then speaks of the real mystery that had been hidden for ages and is now revealed by the message to the saints. He says, *"To whom God would make known what is the riches of the glory of this mystery among the Gentiles; which is Christ in you, the hope of glory"* (Colossians 1:27).

Paul's message is that hidden treasures are in Christ. All the children of God, including the Gentiles, have access to those treasures. Paul then reminds them of where their strength lies. *"That their hearts might be comforted, being knit together in love, and unto all riches of the full assurance of understanding, to the acknowledgement of the mystery of God, and of the Father, and of Christ; In whom are hid all the treasures of wisdom and knowledge. And this I say, lest any man should beguile with enticing words ... As ye have therefore received Christ Jesus the Lord, so walk ye in him: Rooted and build up in him, and stablished in the faith, as ye have been taught, abounding therein with thanksgiving. Beware lest any man spoil you through philosophy and vain deceit, after the tradition of men, after the rudiments of the world, and not after Christ. For in him dwelleth all the fullness of the Godhead bodily. And ye are complete in him, which is the head of all principality and power"* (Colossians 2:2–10).

The Gnostics taught that Christ was subordinate to the true godhead and was among the angels to be worshiped. Paul instructs the Colossians that Christ set them free from man's traditions and religious ceremonies, including the propaganda of the Gnostics. Christ set them free by the freedom they now have in Christ. He says, *"And you, being dead in your sins and the uncircumcision of your flesh, hath he quickened together with him, having forgiven you all trespasses; Blotting out the handwriting of ordinances that was against us, which was contrary to us, and took it out of the way, nailing it to his cross; ... Let no man therefore judge you in meat, or in drink, or in respect of an holyday, or of the new moon, or of the sabbath days: Which are a shadow of the things to come; but the body is of Christ. Let no man beguile you of your reward in a voluntary humility and worshipping of angels, intruding into those things which he hath not seen, vainly puffed up by his fleshy mind, ... Wherefore if ye be dead with Christ from the rudiments of the world, why, as though living in the world, are you subject to ordinances, ... after the commandments and doctrines of men?"* (Colossians 2:13–22).

4) Paul closes with instructions about Christian behavior and how we must put emphasis on love: *"If ye then be risen with Christ, seek those things which are above, where Christ sitteth on the right hand of God. Set your affection on things above, not on things on the earth ... put off all these; anger, wrath, malice, blasphemy, filthy communication out of your mouth. Lie not to one another, seeing that ye have put off the old man with his deeds; And have put on the new man, which is renewed in knowledge after the image of him that created him: ... Put on therefore, as the elect of God, holy and beloved, bowels of mercies, kindness, humbleness of mind, meekness, longsuffering; Forbearing one another, and forgiving one*

another, if any man have a quarrel against any: even as Christ forgave you, so also do ye. And above all these things put on charity, which is the bond of perfectness. And let the peace of God rule in your hearts, to the which also ye are called in one body; and be ye thankful. Let the word of Christ dwell in you richly in all wisdom; teaching and admonishing one another in psalms and hymns and spiritual songs, singing with grace in your hearts to the Lord. And whatsoever ye do in word or deed, do all in the name of the Lord Jesus, giving thanks to God and the father by him" (Colossians 3:1–2, 8–17).

Paul's message to the Colossians is a message to the church today. We need to judge ourselves in the light of Christ's instructions given through Paul. Today's church must be careful not to establish traditions and rules that become the definition of Christianity. Tradition has continued to plague the church because man's nature is to create rules and perform religious ceremonies rather than simply to abide in Christ. Paul tells us that nothing more is required than submitting to Jesus, the eternal glory of the preexistent, omnipotent, exalted, and eternal Son of God.

The key verse:

Colossians 2:8: *"Beware lest any man spoil you through philosophy and vain deceit, after the tradition of men, after the rudiments of the world, and not after Christ."*

1 THESSALONIANS

Paul's letter to the Thessalonian church is the earliest of his recorded letters, written around AD 50. After being called to Macedonia through a vision while on his second missionary journey in Asia Minor, he went first to Philippi, and then on to Thessalonica. However, he was forced to leave Thessalonica under the threat of Jewish leaders that objected to his message, and shortly thereafter wrote the letter from Corinth.

Paul's experience in Thessalonica was most confrontational. Although his message was directed at both Jews and Gentiles, his presentation of the gospel message was the most challenging to those in the Jewish audience because in Christ the Messiah had come and Jewish tradition and law were superseded by the new covenant.

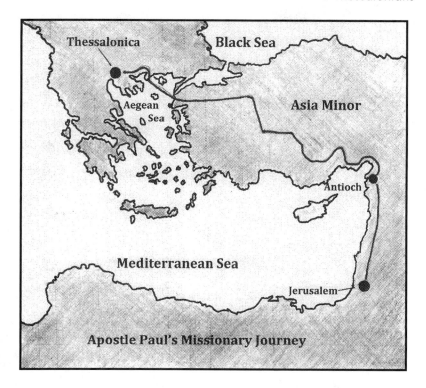

Upon reaching Thessalonica, Paul had reasoned with the Jews in the synagogue on three Sabbath days and taught about the scriptures and Jesus as the Messiah. Some of the Jews believed and were converted, but other Jews rejected his message and caused an uproar (Acts 17:1–9), because the gospel Paul was teaching included the Gentiles and proclaimed that Christians weren't obligated to observe the law. Upon the threat to their lives, Paul and Silas left under nightfall before trouble escalated further. They traveled to Berea, Athens, and then to Corinth.

It appears that the church in Thessalonica had been established before their missionary journey to Macedonia, but Paul and Silas by the power of the Holy Spirit certainly expanded the number of believers during their visit. They had preached the gospel message and won over many Greeks who previously had worshiped heathen idols. Consequently the letter to the Thessalonians was meant to commend them for their faithfulness to the gospel and to advance their faith further. Their devotion to Christ was already well known throughout the region.

Paul writes: "*Remembering without ceasing your work of faith, and labour of love, and patience of hope in our Lord Jesus Christ, in the sight of God and our Father; … So that ye were ensamples to all that believe in Macedonia and Achaia … and how ye turned to God from idols to serve the living and true God; And to wait for his Son from heaven, whom he raised from the dead, even Jesus, which delivered us from the wrath to come*" (1 Thessalonians 1:3, 7, 9–10).

It is apparent, therefore, that Paul, now in Corinth, takes this opportunity by letter to say the things he would have given more emphasis to had he remained longer in Thessalonica. He writes to:

(1) confirm their foundation of faith, (2) to exhort them to go on in holiness, and (3) to comfort them concerning those asleep in Christ.

1) Paul confirms it was a matter of reality that the gospel was the foundation of faith among these believers. They had accepted Christ, and because of that, the Thessalonica Christians were being persecuted. But it was also the source of the apostle's joy, as he commented, *"For ye also have suffered like things of your own countrymen, even as they have of the Jews: Who both killed the Lord Jesus, and their own prophets, and have persecuted us; and they please not God, ... For what is our hope, or joy, or crown of rejoicing? Are not even ye in the presence of our Lord Jesus Christ at his coming? For ye are our glory and joy"* (1 Thessalonians 2:14–20).

Because the Thessalonians were faithful followers of Christ and their faith was known throughout the region, upon the return of Christ, they would be the source of the apostles' glory and joy as testimony of their missionary success. After Paul and Silas had fled from Thessalonica by night, they sent Timothy back to assure the believers that they were safe even though persecuted and to encourage the Thessalonians to remain faithful.

Paul wrote in his letter how encouraged he was: *"Therefore, brethren, we were comforted over you in all our affliction and distress by your faith: For now we live, if ye stand fast in the Lord. For what thanks can we render to God again for you, for all the joy wherewith we joy for your sakes before our God; Night and day praying exceedingly that we might see your face, and might prefect that which is lacking in your faith? … And the Lord make you to increase and abound in love one toward another, and toward all men, even as we do toward you: To the end he may stablish your hearts unblameable in holiness before God"* (1 Thessalonians 3:7–13).

2) Paul was seemingly aware that the believers had an issue about morality, so he addresses their concern with emphasis on strengthening their faith in God through spiritual growth in holiness, that they may be blameless and holy in the presence of God upon Christ's return: *"Furthermore then we beseech you, brethren, and exhort you by the Lord Jesus, that as ye have received of us how ye ought to walk and to please God, so ye would abound more and more. For ye know what commandments we gave you by the Lord Jesus. For this is the will of God, even your sanctification, that ye should abstain from*

fornication: That every one of you should know how to possess his vessel in sanctification and honour; Not in the lust of concupiscence, even as the Gentiles which know not God: That no man go beyond and defraud his brother in any matter: because that the Lord is the avenger of all such, as we also have forewarned you and testified. For God hath not called us unto uncleanness, but unto holiness. He therefore that despiseth, despiseth not man, but God, who hath also given unto us his holy Spirit" (1 Thessalonians 4:1–8).

Paul then emphasizes the basic element from which holiness matures, which is love: *"But as touching brotherly love ye need not that I write unto you: for ye yourselves are taught of God to love one another. And indeed ye do it toward all the brethren which are in all Macedonia: but we beseech you, brethren, that ye increase more and more; And that ye study to be quiet, and to do your own business, and to work with your own hands, as we commanded you; That ye may walk honestly toward them that are without, and that ye may have lack of nothing"* (1 Thessalonians 4:9–12).

3) Paul then addresses the question about those asleep in Christ. Apparently the Thessalonians were under the impression that believers who

died prior to Christ's return would in some way lose out on the blessing of the resurrection, and they grieved for them. But Paul reassured them that Christians who passed on would actually be with Christ on his return and enjoy the blessing of resurrection: *"But I would not have you to be ignorant, brethren, concerning them which are asleep, that ye sorrow not, even as others which have no hope. For if we believe that Jesus died and rose again, even so them also which sleep in Jesus will God bring with him. For this we say unto you by the word of the Lord, that we which are alive and remain unto the coming of the Lord shall not prevent them which are asleep. For the Lord himself shall descend from heaven with a shout, with the voice of the archangel, and with the trump of God: and the dead in Christ shall rise first: Then we which are alive and remain shall be caught up together with them in the clouds, to meet the Lord in the air: and so shall we ever be with the Lord. Wherefore comfort one another with these words"* (1 Thessalonians 4:13-18).

Paul continues to address their concerns, which must have included the question about when the Lord would return: *"But of the times and the seasons, brethren, ye have no need that I write unto you. For yourselves know perfectly that the day of the Lord so cometh as a thief in the night.*

For when they shall say, Peace and safety; then sudden destruction cometh upon them, as travail upon a woman with child; and they shall not escape. But ye, brethren, are not in darkness, that that day should overtake you as a thief. Ye are all the children of light, and the children of the day: we are not of the night, nor of darkness. Therefore, let us not sleep, as do others; but let us watch and be sober. For they that sleep sleep in the night; and they that be drunken are drunken in the night. But let us, who are of the day, be sober, putting on the breastplate of faith and love; and for an helmet, the hope of salvation. For God hath not appointed us to wrath, but to obtain salvation by our Lord Jesus Christ, Who died for us, that, whether we wake or sleep, we should live together with him. Wherefore comfort yourselves together, and edify one another, even as also ye do" (1 Thessalonians 5:1–11).

Paul finishes his letter by encouraging the Thessalonians to respect God's servants and live out their faith. He says, *"And we beseech you, brethren, to know them which labour among you, and are over you in the Lord, and admonish you;*

And to esteem them very highly in love for their work's sake. And be at peace among yourselves. Now we exhort you, brethren, warn them that are unruly, comfort the feebleminded, support the weak, be patient toward all men. See that none render evil for evil unto any man; but ever follow that which is good, both among yourselves, and to all men. Rejoice evermore. Pray without ceasing. In every thing give thanks: for this is the will of God in Christ Jesus concerning you. Quench not the Spirit. Despise not prophesyings. Prove all things; hold fast that which is good. Abstain from all appearance of evil. And the very God of peace sanctify you wholly; And I pray God your whole spirit and soul and body be preserved blameless unto the coming of our Lord Jesus Christ. Faithful is he that calleth you, who also will do it" (1 Thessalonians 5:12–24).

The letter to the Thessalonians was written in recognition of the faith they possessed and displayed as a testimony to others, although they were relatively new in the faith. Since they were Christians new in the faith, Paul wanted to make sure they continued in their spiritual journey to a maturity in holiness (total commitment of their lives to Christ) and thus dedicate their lives to abiding in the gospel of Christ. He instructed them with reference to the behavior that would accompany such commitment, with the understanding that such behavior is by nature a by-product of holiness.

Throughout his epistles Paul reiterates the importance that God places on the faith of his children. He says leave the secular world and its enticements behind and concentrate on our growth spiritually in readiness to serve God and in anticipation of the eternity he has prepared for us.

The key verse:

1 Thessalonians 5:24: *"Faithful is he that calleth you, who also will do it."*

2 THESSALONIANS

The second epistle to the Thessalonians was written shortly after the first, also from Corinth. It appears that the church adherents mistakenly believed that the "day of the Lord," or the final judgment, was upon them. Remember in 1 Thessalonians 4:17 Paul told the Thessalonians that at the second coming of Christ, *"Then we which are alive and remain shall be caught up together with them in the clouds, to meet the Lord in the air."* Therefore the Thessalonica converts originally thought they would be among those caught up with Christ prior to the judgment. However, when they were erroneously told, either by a person or in a letter falsely said to have come from Paul, that the day of the Lord had already come, they were shaken with the thought that the persecution they were experiencing was part of the severe judgment of the "great and terrible day of the Lord" from which they had expected to be delivered. Because of their uncertainty about what was going on, in their answer to Paul's first letter, they posed the question, "Have we been passed over?"

So Paul answered with his second letter and starts out by again recognizing their faith: *"Grace unto you, and peace, from God our Father and the Lord Jesus Christ. We are bound to thank God always for you, brethren, as it is meet, because that your faith growth exceedingly, and the charity of every one of you all toward each other aboundeth; So that we ourselves glory in you in the churches of God for your patience and faith in all your persecutions and tribulations that ye endure"* (2 Thessalonians 1:2–4).

Paul then prefaces his answer to the question posed about the second coming of Christ and judgment with a statement that they can rest assured that they will have reparation for their tribulation, and those false teachers will face God's judgment for their unbelief and persecution of those of faith. Paul assures them, *"Ye may be counted worthy of the kingdom of God, for which ye also suffer: Seeing it is a righteous thing with God to recompense tribulation to them that trouble you; And to you who are troubled rest with us, when the Lord Jesus shall be revealed from heaven with his mighty angels, In flaming fire taking vengeance on them that know not God, and that obey not the gospel of our Lord Jesus Christ: Who shall be punished with everlasting destruction from the presence of the Lord, and from the glory of his power; When he shall come to be glorified in his saints, and to be admired in all them that believe (because our testimony among you was believed) in that day"* (2 Thessalonians 1:5–10).

Paul further emphasizes the fact that the Thessalonica converts still have a mission to perform for the Lord as his servants. This was not consistent with the fraudulent message that the day of the Lord had come.

"Wherefore also we pray always for you, that our God would count you worthy of this calling, and fulfill all the good pleasure of his goodness, and the work of faith with power: That the name of our Lord Jesus Christ may be glorified in you, and ye in him, according to the grace of our God and the Lord Jesus Christ" (2 Thessalonians 1:11–12).

Paul then addresses the question he received from them about Christ's return and their status in the Lord. He assures them that certain things have yet to occur and must come to pass before that day comes: *"That ye be not soon shaken in mind, or be troubled, neither by spirit, nor by word, nor by letter as from us, as that the day of Christ is at hand. Let no man deceive you by any means: for that day shall not come, except there come a falling away first, and that man of sin be revealed, the son of perdition; Who opposeth and exalteth himself above all that is called God, or that is worshiped; so that he as God sitteth in the temple of God, shewing himself that he is God. Remember ye not, that, when I was yet with you, I told you these things? And now ye know what withholdeth that he might be revealed in his time. For the mystery of iniquity doth already work: only he who now letteth will let, until he be taken out of the way"* (2 Thessalonians 2:1–7). Paul told them that the antichrist was not yet revealed because the Holy Spirit was holding him back until the proper time, and that time was not yet here.

But Paul continues with his explanation that when the right time comes the Holy Spirit's restraint will be removed and the antichrist will be exposed with the consequence of his destruction: *"And then shall that Wicked be revealed, whom the Lord shall consume with the spirit of his mouth, and*

*shall destroy with the brightness of his coming:
Even him, whose coming is after the working of
Satan with all power and signs and lying wonders,
And with all deceivableness of unrighteousness
in them that perish; because they received not
the love of the truth, that they might be saved.
And for this cause God shall send them strong
delusion, that they should believe a lie: That
they all might be damned who believed not the
truth, but had pleasure in unrighteousness"*
(2 Thessalonians 2:8–12).

Then Paul tells the Thessalonians that he thanks
God for them as brothers loved by the Lord
because from the beginning God chose them to
be saved through the sanctifying work of the Spirit
and through belief in the truth. He encouraged
them to stand firm and hold to the teachings that
were passed on to them. He said that God, who
by grace brought them eternal encouragement,
would be a strength for them in every good deed
and word.

Further, since the Thessalonians believed that
the time of Christ's return was imminent, some of
them were not working but simply waiting for the
event. Their thinking must have been, *Why should
I work if tomorrow Christ is returning?* But since

Paul had just written that Christ's return was yet in the future, he admonished them to get back to work. He told them to avoid those who don't live according to the apostles' teaching and to keep away from idle brothers.

It appears that Paul must have felt that some of those waiting were using Christ's return as an excuse not to work. But since they were living off of others, it was apparent that this was becoming a problem in their testimony. How could they be effective witnesses for Christ if they were seen as loafers, or worse, if they were using it as an outright pretense for not working? Thus, he became more animated in his admonishment about the situation and gave them this rule: "*If any would not work, neither should he eat*" (2 Thessalonians 3:10).

And then Paul went on with more definitive language about the problem: "*For we hear that there are some which walk among you disorderly, working not at all, but are busybodies. Now them that are such we command and exhort by our Lord Jesus Christ, that with quietness they work, and eat their own bread. But ye, brethren, be not weary in well doing. And if any man obey not our word by this epistle, note that man, and have no company with him, that he may be ashamed. Yet count him not as an enemy, but admonish him as a brother"* (2 Thessalonians 3:11–15).

Paul's letter to the Thessalonians addressed their question about the timing of Christ's return. The answer was that certain things had to happen first that included the appearing of the antichrist, who will proclaim himself as God and actually set himself up in God's temple. This indicates that a world leader will arise under Satan's dominion who, in conjunction with other political factions, will deceive the world as a political "rock star." He will attract the veneration of the masses to such an extent that he will rise to the level of a man-god. It also suggests that the temple in Jerusalem will be rebuilt and function to the extent that the antichrist will take it over as his spiritual throne. We do not know how that will happen, but we do know that it is prophesied in Daniel and in Revelation, and that it will come to pass when God initiates the time. As Christ said in Mark 13:32, *"But of that day and that hour knoweth no man, no, not the angels which are in heaven, neither the Son, but the Father."* Only God the Father knows the timing of end times.

It is also noteworthy that 2 Thessalonians provides insight about the question that has continued among Bible scholars even to the present day regarding the point at which the church will be raptured (i.e., pre- or post-millennium). It appears that Paul tells us that Christians will be taken up, delivered, and gathered unto Christ before the great and terrible tribulation, which suggests that it will be pre-millennial, but that assumes the great and terrible tribulation refers to Armageddon. We are to watch and to be ready.

The key verse:

2 Thessalonians 3:3: *"But the Lord is faithful, who shall stablish you, and keep you from evil."*

PASTORAL EPISTLES

The pastoral epistles are letters that Paul wrote to those he called his sons after the common faith, Timothy and Titus. He wrote to instruct them about church order and proper behavior. Paul was in prison, and some of his followers were leaving. Some left because they had a misunderstanding with Paul, or they chose not to continue in their rigorous commitment of service. But others had been sent on missions to reach the lost and to strengthen the church. Timothy and Titus were of the latter, assisting Paul in his work to instruct the churches.

Philemon has been included in the pastoral epistles because of the example of brotherly love. Philemon was a slave owner, and his slave, Onesimus, had run away to Rome. Paul had met Onesimus and converted him to Christ, and Paul was writing to let Philemon know his slave was returning as a new man. These letters provide the standards that the present church should follow, and to judge themselves accordingly.

1 TIMOTHY

The letter is said to have been written just before Paul was imprisoned in Rome. He had left Timothy in Ephesus when Paul continued on his journey to Macedonia. Paul's instructions were to make sure the body of believers taught sound doctrine and not to be engrossed in fables and endless discussions about genealogies. Paul was saying that some of the people at Ephesus, who were probably converted Jews, were distorting the love of Christ and were involved in what Paul called "vain jangling." They wanted to teach the law, but Paul said the law wasn't for the good man, but for the wicked and the unlawful. In other words, the law did not apply to the new covenant for the children of God in the glorious gospel committed to Paul's trust. And Paul thanked God who forgave him when, as a Pharisee, he had persecuted believers in Christ, because Paul did those things ignorantly in unbelief. Paul gave the faithful saying, *"Christ Jesus came into the world to save sinners; of whom I am chief"* (1 Timothy 1:15). Paul says that he, the worst of sinners, was shown mercy that our Lord might display his unlimited patience as an example for those who would believe in our Jesus and receive the gift of eternal life by the grace of God.

Paul also gave Timothy instructions on providing effective leadership, including five areas that were important in his mission to assist in church administration, involving: (1) faith warfare, (2) leadership requirements, (3) avoiding tradition, (4) respectful obligations, and (5) avoiding worldliness.

1) In the first Paul urged Timothy to press on in his warfare concerning faith. Paul says to Timothy, *"I exhort therefore, that, first of all, supplications, prayers, intercessions, and giving of thanks, be made for all men; For kings, and for all that are in authority; that we may lead a quiet and peaceful life in all godliness and honesty. For this is good and acceptable in the sight of God our Saviour; Who will have all men to be saved, and to come unto the knowledge of the truth. For there is one God, and one mediator between God and men, the*

man Christ Jesus; Who gave himself a ransom for all, to be testified in due time" (1 Timothy 2:1–6). This is noteworthy and confirms that all were included in Christ's redemptive purpose.

Then he says, *"I will therefore that men pray every where, lifting up holy hands, without wrath and doubting. In like manner also, that women adorn themselves in modest apparel, ... not with broided hair, or gold, or pearls, or costly array; But (which becometh women professing godliness) with good works. ... But I suffer not a woman to teach, nor to usurp authority over the man, but to be in silence"* (1 Timothy 2:8–12).

It is interesting that Paul says, *"I will."* It appears that Paul as an apostle is giving instructions that he feels are appropriate for church order, but he does not say it is *"God's will."* This may be Paul's assessment reflecting the customs of that period, rather than Christian doctrine for all time, since God has certainly blessed the women missionaries who have reached the lost and the wonderful work women have performed for the church. There is no question, however, that God meant for men to fulfill their responsibility in God's service, and sadly that has not been the rule in many cases. Women have filled the void.

2) Paul then covers the requirements of church leaders, starting with a bishop, referring to the leader of the congregation or the pastor: *"A bishop then must be blameless, the husband of one wife, vigilant, sober, of good behavior, given to hospitality; apt to teach; Not given to wine, no striker, not greedy of filthy lucre; but patient, not a brawler, not covetous; One that ruleth well his own house, having his children in subjection with all gravity; ... Not a novice, ... must have a good report of them which are without; less he fall into reproach and the snare of the devil"* (1 Timothy 3:2–7).

Paul also gives the instructions for a deacon, and that refers to those who serve under the bishop. *"Likewise must the deacons be grave, not double tongued, not given to much wine, not greedy of filthy lucre; Holding the mystery of the faith in a pure conscience. And let these also first be proved; then let them use the office of a deacon, being found blameless ... Let the deacons be the husbands of one wife, ruling their children and their own houses well"* (1 Timothy 3:8–12).

Those who perform well in this capacity are said to purchase or to acquire a good degree and boldness in the faith. Paul says that a wife of a deacon must also be mature, not slanderous, sober, and faithful in all things. He stipulates that this is how to behave in the house of God, the church of the living God, the pillar and ground of the truth. Great is the mystery of godliness.

3) Paul relates to Timothy that in latter times many will depart from the faith and preach things of man, such as forbidding to marry and abstaining from meats. *"For every creature of God is good, and nothing to be refused, if it be received with thanksgiving: For it is sanctified by the word of God and prayer ... put the brethren in remembrance of these things, ... refuse profane and old wives' fables, and exercise thyself rather unto godliness ... profitable unto all things, having promise of the life that now is, and of that which is to come ... Neglect not the gift that is in thee, ... Meditate upon these things; give thyself wholly to them; that thy profiting may appear to all"* (1 Timothy 4:4–15).

4) Then Paul tells Timothy not to rebuke an elder, but treat him as a father, the younger men as brothers, the elder women as a mother, and the younger as sisters with all purity and then to honor widows. Those women over sixty years and without children are to be looked after in supplementation

and prayer. Those who are not desolate and have children should be looked after by the children or other relatives. Young widows should remarry and start over again, and not burden the church in order to reserve the assistance for those who are really in need.

Regarding compensation for the pastor, he should be given double honor when he does well and works in the word and doctrine of Christ. Don't accept an accusation against a pastor unless there are two or three witnesses, and then rebuke him in front of the body, so others may fear. Timothy was told to observe these things without partiality and show no favoritism. Think things through before acting, and drink a little wine to maintain good health.

5) Paul cautions Timothy to withdraw from those who are worldly. He tells him to instruct those Christians under the yolk of a master or slaves to honor the master so that the name of God and his doctrine not be blasphemed. Also Christian masters are to honor their servants because they are partakers of the faith.

He says to withdraw from those who do not act accordingly. Godliness with contentment is great gain because we came into this world with nothing and will leave with nothing. The love of money is the root of all evil, and Paul says that such covetousness will pierce the guilty with many sorrows. Timothy is to flee from these things and follow after love, faith, righteousness, godliness, patience, and meekness. He tells him to instruct the rich to trust only in the living God, not uncertain riches, but to do good and be rich in good works and ready to give, providing their foundation against the times to come, and prepare for eternal life. Paul tells him: *"Fight the good fight of faith, lay hold on eternal life, whereunto thou art also called, and hast professed a good profession before many witnesses"* (1 Timothy 6:12).

The key verse:

1 Timothy 3:15: *"That you mayest know how thou oughtest to behave thyself in the house of the God, which is the church of the living God, the pillar and ground of the truth."*

2 TIMOTHY

This epistle to Timothy *"my beloved son"* was written shortly before Paul's martyrdom and is believed to be his last written words. Some of the Asian churches had started to turn away from the doctrines of grace taught by Paul. He now wrote to instruct Timothy in his walk and testimony as a servant of Christ in the day of apostasy. But he also wrote in justification of his own service and commitment to God. This is a precious letter delineating the Christian walk that applies timelessly to the Christian in this present world. Five areas were delineated; (1) faithful to commitment, (2) dedicated walk, (3) apostasy, (4) inspired scripture, and (5) his salutation.

1) Paul starts by complimenting Timothy for his faith that was also seen in Timothy's mother and grandmother. He tells him to stir up the gift

that was given to him by the laying on of Paul's hands. He also says that God didn't give us the spirit of fear, but of power and of love and a sound mind. Paul says, *"Be not thou therefore ashamed of the testimony of our Lord, nor of me his prisoner: but be thou partaker of the afflictions of the gospel according to the power of God; Who hath saved us, and called us with an holy calling, not according to our works, but according to his own purpose and grace, which was given us in Christ Jesus before the world began, But is now made manifest by the appearing of our Savior Jesus Christ, who hath abolished death, and hath brought life and immortality to light through the gospel"* (2 Timothy 1:8–10). These are instructive words that present the essence of salvation by grace and the justification for the ministry that Timothy was to pursue.

For that cause Paul, too, was called as a preacher, as an apostle, and as a teacher of the Gentiles, for which he suffered. He then gives that famous verse of 2 Timothy 1:12: *"Nevertheless I am not ashamed: for I know whom I have believed, and am persuaded that he is able to keep that which I have committed unto him against that day."* He charges Timothy to keep that good thing which was committed unto him by the Holly Spirit and dwells within the believer.

2) Regarding the walk of the believer who is committed to serve, Paul tells Timothy to be strong in the grace that is in Christ Jesus, and to teach that which Paul taught and endure hardness. No man who wars for Christ entangles himself in the affairs of this life. He is to strive lawfully and use the understanding that the Lord gave him. Paul says, *"Therefore I endure all things for the elect's sakes, that they may also obtain the salvation which is in Christ Jesus with eternal glory ... if we be dead with him, we shall also live with him: If we suffer, we shall also reign with him: if we deny him, he also will deny us"* (2 Timothy 2:10–12).

Paul continues: *"Study to shew thyself approved unto God, a workman that needeth not to be ashamed, rightly dividing the word of truth. But shun profane and vain babblings: for they will increase unto more ungodliness. ... the foundation of God standeth sure, having this seal, The Lord knoweth them that are his. And, Let every one that nameth the name of Christ depart from iniquity. But in a great house there are not only vessels of gold and of silver, but also of wood and of earth; and some to honour, and some to dishonor. If a man therefore purge himself from these, he shall be a vessel unto honour, sanctified, and meet for the master's use, and prepared for every good work. Flee also youthful lusts: but follow righteousness, faith, charity, peace, with them that call on the Lord out of a pure heart. But foolish and unlearned questions avoid, knowing that they do gender strifes. And the servant of the Lord must not strive; but be gentle unto all men, apt to teach, patient, In meekness instructing those that oppose themselves; if God peradventure will give them repentance to the acknowledging of the truth; And that they may recover themselves out of the snare of the devil, who are taken captive by him at his will"* (2 Timothy 2:15–26).

3) Then Paul turns to the subject of apostasy in latter times when men will be lovers of themselves and pleasures more than lovers of God. They will have a form of godliness but will deny the power of God. Paul says to turn away from them. They will pursue learning but will not be able to come to the knowledge of the truth.

Paul's words are prophetic. We see that situation occurring today, a form of godliness, but they deny Christ as God and his power and his redeeming grace, and their followers are stillborn in the devil's snare.

4) Paul then turns to the inspired word. He encourages Timothy to continue in his knowledge of those things he has learned. He says, *"All scripture is given by inspiration of God, and is profitable for doctrine, for reproof, for correction, for instruction in righteousness: That the man of God may be perfect, thoroughly furnished unto all good works"* (2 Timothy 3:16–17).

So Paul emphasizes that those made perfect in the eyes of God by the cleansing blood of Jesus will be sustained in good works by the instructions of the scriptures. He charges Timothy, *"Preach the word; be instant in season, out of season; reprove, rebuke, exhort with all longsuffering and doctrine. For the time will come when they will not endure sound doctrine; but after their own lusts shall they heap to themselves teachers, having itching ears; And they shall turn away their ears from the truth, and shall be turned unto fables. But watch thou in all things, endure afflictions, do the work of an evangelist, make full proof of thy ministry"* (2 Timothy 4:2–5).

5) Paul finishes with his salutation. He knows his end is at hand. He says, *"For I am now ready to be offered, and the time of my departure is at hand. I have fought a good fight, I have finished my course, I have kept the faith: Henceforth there is laid up for me a crown of righteousness, which the Lord, the righteous judge, shall give me at that day: and not to me only, but unto all them also that love his appearing"* (2 Timothy 4:6–8).

The key verse:

2 Timothy 4:7: *"I have fought a good fight, I have finished my course, I have kept the faith."*

TITUS

The letter to Titus is very similar to 1 Timothy where the subject is about church order. The emphasis in Timothy was sound doctrine, whereas in Titus the subject is more on divine order of the local churches. In this case Paul had left Titus in Crete to help establish the order of God's house and to ordain elders or preachers in the assemblies. The requirements of the elders were the same as given in 1 Timothy and will not be repeated here. Paul emphasizes the need to provide sound doctrine because there were many who proclaimed false doctrine for financial benefit. Paul emphasizes three points: (1) good behavior, (2) principle of love, and (3) to reject heretics.

1) Paul reiterates to Titus that which he told Timothy regarding good behavior that becomes

holiness—that older men and women should be sober, grave, temperate, and sound in faith and show charity, and patience. They should not be given to much wine, not false accusers. Young men and women should also be sober and should love their children and care for each other. In all cases respect authority and deny ungodliness and worldly lusts. Paul says that such behavior will cause those who are contrary to your preaching to feel ashamed because they will have no evil thing to say of you.

2) Paul then claims the principle of God's love: *"Not by works of righteousness which we have done, but according to his mercy he saved us, by the washing of regeneration, and renewing of the Holy Ghost; Which he shed on us abundantly through Jesus Christ our Saviour; That being justified by his grace, we should be made heirs according to the hope of eternal life. This is a faithful saying, and these things I will that thou affirm constantly, that they which have believed in God might be careful to maintain good works. These things are good and profitable unto men"* (Titus 3:5–8).

3) Paul ends by saying that we are to reject a man who is a heretic after the first and second

admonition. Such a person is subverted and sins willfully and thus condemns himself.

The key verse:

Titus 3:7: *"That being justified by his grace, we should be made heirs according to the hope of eternal life."*

PHILEMON

Onesimus was a slave who apparently stole from his master, Philemon, and ran away to Rome. But Paul somehow met him, and Onesimus was converted and became a loving brother to Paul. Onesimus was now returning to his master, and Paul wrote a letter that was to accompany him, asking Philemon, who was a believer and a dear friend of Paul, to accept him back as a brother in Christ. The essence of Paul's letter is a letter of compassion in the love of Christ.

"Unto Philemon our dearly beloved, and fellow-laborer ... I beseech thee for my son Onesimus, whom I have begotten in my bonds: Which in time past was to thee unprofitable, but now profitable to thee and to me: Whom I have sent again; thou therefore receive him, that is my own bowels: Whom I would have retained with me,

that in thy stead he might have ministered unto me in the bonds of the gospel: But without thy mind would I do nothing; that thy benefit should not be as it were of necessity, but willingly. For perhaps he therefore departed for a season, that thou shouldest receive him for ever; Not now as a servant, but above a servant, a brother beloved, especially to me, but how much more unto thee, both in the flesh, and in the Lord? If thou count me therefore a partner, receive him as myself" (Philemon 1:10–17).

HEBREWS

Hebrews is a unique letter. It is unique in its intent. It has none of the greetings or salutations that were characteristic of the other of Paul's New Testament letters and appears more as a lecture, except for the last few verses in reference to the letter itself. Although there has been controversy about the author of Hebrews, there are those scholars that feel the evidence points to Paul, also evident in the last verses of the letter. For this reason, Hebrews is included in this synopsis of Paul's epistles.

It was written sometime prior to AD 70 and is entitled "Hebrews" because it is addressed specifically to Jewish Christians. That point is critical in understanding the letter. The intent had a twofold purpose. First, it was to show those wavering in their profession of belief in Christ that the old covenant had come to an end by Christ having fulfilled the law. That in itself was a monumental issue in Jewish thought when the law had been so basic in their faith.

Second, the exhortation reveals the ever-present danger to the Jewish professed believers of either lapsing back into Judaism or falling short of true faith in Jesus Christ. Knowing who the intended audience was provides a better understanding of the letter and the resolution to the meaning of certain passages that have been controversial when taken out of the context of the message to the intended recipients, the Jewish professed believers in Christ.

The letter points out five issues relevant to the Jews' understanding of their position in Christ:

(1) the supremacy of Christ, (2), the promised land, (3) duplicity of tradition, (4) the high priest, and (5) the new covenant.

1) The letter starts out making the very point the Jews had to first understand, which was that Jesus Christ was superior to Moses and the prophets, a comparison that would be most significant to them. They were told that God never said to an angel, *"Thou art my Son,"* but he says, *"And let all*

the angels of God worship him. ... But unto the Son he saith, Thy throne, O God, is forever and ever: a sceptre of righteousness is a sceptre of thy kingdom ... And, Thou, Lord, in the beginning hast laid the foundations of the earth; and the heavens are the works of thine hands: They shall perish; ... but thou art the same, and thy years shall not fail" (Hebrews 1:5–12).

They were told that they should pay all the more heed to what they were being taught for fear of drifting away from their course. If the angels are punished for disobedience, what escape can there be for us if we ignore a deliverance so great? The Jewish Christians were told that everything is in subjection to the Lord Jesus Christ. They were to realize that Christ as God himself, manifest as the Son in the form of man, had provided salvation to the Jews by the ultimate sacrifice.

The Jewish believers were told, *"For it became him, for whom are all things, and by whom are all things, in bringing many sons unto glory, to make the captain of their salvation perfect through sufferings"* (Hebrews 2:10).

Christ as that perfect sacrifice by his death on the cross and resurrection into life did away with the purpose for all the sacrifices the Jews had performed under the law of Moses. As the new covenant, he came as the deliverer and took unto himself all those who are the sons of Abraham.

This was the message that the Jewish professed Christians teetering between Christ and the law could understand. There was no middle ground. Christ had fulfilled the law, and the sons of Abraham were those who were made righteous through the blood of Christ. They were told that Christ is greater than Moses and not to be stubborn by worldly judgment and unbelief, as their forefathers were after their unwillingness to enter the Promised Land and died in the desert, but to encourage one another to keep their original confidence in Christ firm to the end.

2) The Promised Land was a type of "rest" that God entered on the seventh day as he rested after the creation. God's rest is that place of eternal peace where life has no end and God's promises come to pass in his heavenly kingdom. Those who were uncertain were told that while the promise of entering God's rest remains open, don't miss the opportunity to enter. They have heard the good news as their forefathers heard in times past, but in them the message did no good because they had no mixture of faith with the hearing.

That rest remains open to those who, by faith, accept God's promises for themselves and are delivered from the curse of sin. Some of those who professed Christ had not actually entered that rest because they felt observing the law should still be a component of their faith. But they were told that the sacrifices pertaining to the law were only a shadow of which Christ was the substance. As the Messiah, Christ supplanted the law, and being made perfect, Christ was the author of eternal salvation unto all who obey him. Those who had professed a faith in Christ but clung to the law must recognize their middle-ground position and instead endeavor to enter that rest, lest they fall after the same example of their forefathers' unbelief.

3) It was then said to this group of Hebrews that it was difficult to explain the deeper things of God because they were yet in need of milk instead of solid food. We as Christians should not be laying over again the foundations of faith in God and repentance from the deadness of our former ways but to pursue unto perfection after Christ.

The letter went on to exemplify the situation that those middle-ground Jews faced: *"For it is impossible for those who were once enlightened, and have tasted of the heavenly gift, and were made partakers of the Holy Ghost, And have tasted the good word of God, and the powers of the world to come, If they shall fall away, to renew them again unto repentance; seeing they crucify to themselves the Son of God afresh and put him to an open shame"* (Hebrews 6:4–6).

Those Jews who had toyed with a faith in Christ had tasted the heavenly gift and observed the evidence of the Holy Spirit, had fallen away from grasping the truth of salvation because they continued to rely on the sacrificial tradition of the law. The consequence of that problem was then pointed out. It was impossible to bring those individuals to Christ because their reliance on the law was to continue the sacrifice of Christ as though it was the ongoing sacrificial offerings for their sins after the tradition of the Levitical priesthood.

4) The point about the Levitical priesthood would have had special meaning to the Jews. In the Levitical priesthood, the high priest would enter the Holy of Holies of the sanctuary God first instructed Moses to build in the desert, and later in Solomon's temple, once a year to give sacrifices for sin, including those of the priest

himself. But Christ is identified by God as the high priest after the order of Melchisedec (Genesis 14:18), who was King of righteousness, the King of Peace, the High Priest of God: *"Without father, without mother, without descent, having neither beginning of days, nor end of life; but made like unto the Son of God; abideth a priest continually"* (Hebrews 7:3).

God said of Jesus, *"Thou art a priest for ever after the order of Melchisedec"* (Hebrews 7:17). This was not the priesthood in the succession of Aaron of the tribe of Levi of the old covenant, but a higher priesthood. Abraham had given tithes to Melchisedec, recognizing his greatness. Therefore, while the Levitical priesthood was a line of succession of priests because of death, and involved continued offering of animal sacrifices for the sins committed by the Jews, including their own, Christ was identified as a higher priest, alive forever, who has no sin, who was the ultimate and conclusive sacrifice. Christ's sacrifice is sufficient for the redemption of all sin for all time.

"And it is yet far more evident, for that after the similitude of Melchisedec there ariseth another priest, Who is made, not after the law of the carnal commandment, but after the power of an endless

life. For he testifieth, Thou art a priest for ever after the order of Melchisedec. ... For the law made nothing perfect, but the bringing in of a better hope did: by the which we draw nigh unto God" (Hebrews 7:15–19).

5) The Son who was made perfect is perfect now and forever. He supersedes the law, the ordinances, offerings, and various rites of cleansing. Jesus now sits at the right hand of the throne of the Majesty in the heavens. His ministry in the sanctuary and true tabernacle, not built with hands, is far superior to the earthly sanctuary Moses was instructed to build, as is the new covenant that Christ mediates and the promises upon which it is legally secured.

The Lord confirms his intent and says, *"This is the covenant that I will make with them after those days, saith the Lord, I will put my laws into their hearts, and in their minds will I write them; And their sins and iniquities will I remember no more. Now where remission of these is, there is no more offering for sin"* (Hebrews 10:16–18).

The key element in this exhortation is that the Jews as professed believers must realize the fullness of who Christ is, and with that knowledge recognize that he has made the old covenant obsolete with the new covenant promises now to be embedded by faith upon the minds and hearts of believers. If the old covenant had been sufficient, there would have been no need for the new. Sacrifices continued in the old covenant because it was impossible for blood of bulls and goats to take away sin. The old covenant was only a shadow of that which was to come as the new trust between God and his people. The old covenant and its ordinances were compared with the new covenant to show the Jewish Christians that the old ways and traditions had passed away. They were to put their faith now in Jesus as the perfect sacrifice that would remove their sins from the memory of God and render believers perfect in God's eyes. They were to go forward in the faith that was demonstrated by the patriarchs for things not yet seen, and he gave several examples of such faith. They were told not to refuse the voice of God—not to shrink back and be lost because of the severe penalty of those who trample underfoot the Son of God, profane the blood of the covenant by which he was consecrated, and affront God's gracious Spirit.

As with Christians, the Jewish believers were to endure the discipline that a loving God will administer to his children as a loving father corrects his children. *"For whom the Lord loveth he chasteneth, ... for what son is he whom the father chasteneth not?"* (Hebrews 12:6–7). They were to love their fellow Christians, to honor marriage, and to show hospitality. They were not to live for money, and be content with what they have, for God has said, *"I will never leave you or desert you."*

This was a message applicable to all Christians, but in this case most important to those Jewish-professed believers who were tempted to include their traditional reliance upon the law. It was made clear that such a hybrid between the law and Christ was a mockery of Christ and a gross misunderstanding of the purpose for which he came.

The fact of the matter was that by continuing to include the law in their concept of redemption, it was obvious that the Jewish professed believers had a very different and incomplete concept of what the coming of Christ accomplished. They had not accepted fully in their hearts that Christ's sacrifice was for the redemption of man from his sin once and for all time. As explained in Hebrews 6:4–6, those who had professed belief but still depended on the law were unable to realize redemption for their sin by Christ's death, because by keeping the Levitical tradition, those Jews were continuing to sacrifice Christ over and over again, as though his sacrifice lacked sufficient duration to redeem sin for all time.

The message to those Hebrews who had actually surrendered to the gospel of Christ was that they were now free of the law and had received confirmation that they were truly the children of God, because of the ultimate and conclusive sacrifice that God provided for all time. That reality was consistent with the plan of God, and like Paul, the Jews would now have compassion for their kin who had yet to know the sufficiency of Christ.

The key verse:

Hebrews 11:1: *"Now faith is the substance of things hoped for, the evidence of things not seen."*

RETROSPECT

Paul's epistles bring out the basic truths of God's word that apply to the body of believers today as they did during Paul's missionary journeys. The epistles reveal the "gospel of God" that presents the redemptive truth of God's word, the doctrine of grace, faith, and the principles of the new life in Christ. There are some issues in retrospect that should be reemphasized.

In Romans when Paul referred to the rationale of the wise to worship the creatures rather than the creator, his reference has direct application to present-day secular interpretation of science where the source of all that we see and know is attributed only to natural causes, missing the evidence that such causes are only the instruments of the supernatural. Paul says they are foolish when the evidence of creation is all around and should leave no doubt about the existence of the Creator. In their arrogance, the wise of today attribute the knowledge and discoveries of biological and molecular systems to those natural processes, but they are blind to the fact that those processes would not have occurred in the absence of an omnipotent Creator who provided the molecular/ chemical blueprints and mechanisms that made them possible. The natural laws and processes originated with the Creator, and we are foolish to mistake them otherwise.

Several of Paul's epistles refer to the law given to Moses and contrast the old covenant under the law with the new covenant under grace. As Charles Price pointed out in his book *Alive in Christ*, the law is a description of God, and thus the purpose in giving the law to the Jews was to identify righteousness. The law made it obvious that man was incapable of being righteous and thus incapable of being sinless as God was sinless.

Under the new covenant, Christ came as the Son of God and took upon himself the redemption of humankind from all sin by making the ultimate blood sacrifice—his death on the cross in the place of man. That was the Messiah, Christ, taking upon himself the penalty of sin. His resurrection conquered death, and those who by faith take Christ's sacrifice as their own die with him and are raised again into a new life with the promise of forgiveness and eternal life, cleansed of their sins in the eyes of God as they will stand before him.

Charles Price demonstrated how the Christian should see the Ten Commandments as the ten promises in the Spirit of our new life in Christ. By faith we accepted the sacrifice of our savior as our own, and we are righteous in the eyes of God because the indwelling Spirit of Christ is righteous. And when we stumble with sin, the Spirit convicts us of the offense, and we ask for forgiveness, cleansed not by our confession but by the fact that our sins were taken by Christ once and for all. As long as we are in the flesh of this world, we must arm ourselves against the influence of the world, but in the Spirit, we look forward to the new bodies we will acquire at the second coming of Christ and therein realize the perfection in body and spirit, as referenced in Philippians (3:10–16).

The key to a productive and full life in Christ is surrendering our will to the will of God and allowing the Spirit to work though us. Just as the Jews were unable to keep the commandments, Christians are unable to live a righteous life in themselves. To be righteous in the eyes of God, Christians must allow Christ to live within them. It is not what we can do for God but what God can do through us. As Christ said in John 5:19, *"The Son can do nothing of himself, but what he seeth the father do."* Likewise, we can do nothing of ourselves but must through prayer depend on Christ to work through us as individuals and collectively as members of the body, exercising our different gifts for the glory of God (Romans 12:4–6). We are the vessels that God works through to do his will and his good pleasure (Philippians 2:13).

Finally, in Paul's epistles the mystery hidden from the Jews as the chosen people of God was revealed. That mystery was the hidden truth that the Gentiles were included with the children of God, that both Jews and Gentiles would constitute the body of Christ, the true church. The Christian is now the temple of the Holy Spirit (1 Corinthians 3:16), with the Spirit of God dwelling in our hearts rather than in the Holy of Holies of the sanctuary. Consequently, the Christian is the holy residence of the Holy Spirit.

The significance of that revelation cannot be minimized. No longer are the faithful separated from direct access to God, given representation via a high priest in the Holy of Holies of the sanctuary, but now the believer made perfect by the blood of Christ has direct access to God via God's Spirit dwelling within the heart. Such a sober realization should quicken every Christian to walk honoring and respectful of our Lord in all aspects of the lives God has given us. We have a gift beyond all gifts, justified only by the grace of God. We are to be holy in our walk in this world as Jesus is holy, and we can only achieve that holiness by submitting to the Spirit of God and endeavoring to perform in his service. God promised Abraham that *"in thee all the families of the earth shall be blessed"* (Genesis 12:3). That was possible only through the construct of the new covenant. The blessing came through Christ as the redeemer available for all people. The epistles are timeless.

Printed in the United States
By Bookmasters